EIGHT SOVIET COMPOSERS

Gerald Abraham

EIGHT SOVIET
COMPOSERS

GREENWOOD PRESS, PUBLISHERS
WESTPORT, CONNECTICUT

The Library of Congress cataloged this book as follows:

Abraham, Gerald Ernest Heal, 1904–
  Eight Soviet composers ₁by₁ Gerald Abraham. Westport,
Conn., Greenwood Press ₁1970₁

  102 p. music. 23 cm.

  Reprint of the 1943 ed.

  CONTENTS. — Dmitry Shostakovich. — Sergey Prokofiev. — Aram
Khachaturyan.—Lev Knipper.—Vissarion Shebalin.—Dmitry Kabalevsky.—Ivan Dzerzhinsky.—Yury Shaporin.

  1. Composers, Russian. 2. Music—Russia—1917–

ML390.A13 1970   780′.922 [B]   71–106679
ISBN 0–8371–3350–5   MARC

Library of Congress   70 ₁7₁   MN

Originally published in 1943 by Oxford University Press,
London

Reprinted with the permission of Oxford University Press

Reprinted from an original copy in the collections of the
Brooklyn Public Library

Reprinted by Greenwood Press, Inc.

First Greenwood reprinting 1970
Second Greenwood reprinting 1976

Library of Congress Catalog Card Number 71-106679

ISBN 0-8371-3350-5

Printed in the United States of America

CONTENTS

ACKNOWLEDGEMENT

Six of these essays have appeared in slightly different form in *The Monthly Musical Record*, that on Shostakovich in *Horizon*, that on Prokofiev in *The Music Review*, and part of the Introduction in *The Gramophone*, and I offer my grateful thanks to the respective editors for permission to reprint them. My thanks are also due to Dr. A. Aber, of Novello & Co., Ltd., the English agents of the Russian State Music Publishing Company, for kindly allowing me to consult scores otherwise inaccessible.

I. INTRODUCTION

THE AIM of this little book is much less to offer criticism than to give information. Ask any English musician what he knows about the music of our Soviet allies and the odds are about seven to one that he will answer, 'Oh, Shostakovich, you know. And that old chap, Myaskovsky, who writes innumerable symphonies. And the fellow who wrote the steel-foundry thing—Mosolov,' and that he will then, or very soon after, stick. My object is to help him past the sticking point by describing in some detail the careers and work of eight outstanding Soviet composers. It would be easy to add to the number, but these eight are not only, in my view, the most important: they are thoroughly representative of Soviet Russian music as a whole.

There are numerous reasons for our British ignorance of this music: not political prejudice so much as commercial reasons, the chief of them being neglect by the Russians themselves to push the sales of their scores and gramophone records in Western Europe. This neglect—often infuriating to those of us who have been anxious to get to know the work of Soviet musicians—was by no means entirely due to lack of business sense on the part of the State Publishing house; sheer indifference, I suspect, played a big part— simple indifference to what musicians outside the U.S.S.R. might think. And that leads us straight to the main characteristic of Soviet music, particularly during the last ten years: its self-centredness. Soviet music is self-centred and self-sufficient—but by no means self-satisfied: on the contrary, it is intensely self-critical—because it has a special problem or set of problems to cope with and is exclusively preoccupied with finding the solution. The problem was posed by the Soviet Government, which treats composers very handsomely[1] but, paying the pipers, insists on its right to call the

---

[1] Through the Union of Soviet Composers it commissions from them works for which it pays generously; in addition composers are entitled to performing fees and to payment by the State music-publishers if their works are printed. If the Soviet composer is ill he gets free treatment; if he goes on holiday, he is given help in paying for it (if he needs help). The Government, through the Union of Soviet Composers, may even provide him with

tunes. Being a government of the people, it insists on music for the
people, not music for intellectuals, for those with highly trained
ears and sophisticated tastes. It insists that Soviet music shall be
lyrical and melodious, that it shall be the expression of real feeling,
and of joyous or heroic or optimistic feeling rather than of personal,
subjective brooding. These conditions are quite foreign to our conception of the circumstances in which a creative artist should work
and they have exercised an almost crippling restraint on such
talented musicians]as Shostakovich and Knipper, to say nothing of
their limiting effect on Shebalin, Khachaturyan and many others;
yet the Russian mind loves a problem, and this problem must be
a very congenial one to every Soviet musician. But it is easy to see
how its existence, how the ideal of 'music for the masses', has
tended to make the Soviet musician somewhat indifferent to the
views of his Western colleagues.

However, the Western musician's approach is simplified by the
fact that despite the deliberate efforts of the Soviet authorities to
create a Soviet music *sui generis*, the music of the U.S.S.R. is in
many respects—though with certain qualifications and naturally
with numerous fresh developments—in the tradition of pre-
Revolutionary Russian music. When in 1917 the Revolution barred
the return home of certain Russian musicians who happened to be
abroad and, before long, sent others to join them in exile, Russian
music might easily have lost that invaluable imponderable, 'con-
tinuity of tradition'. It did not, however. And for that fact Russian
musicians have to thank a small group of composers, not men of
the first rank but artists well equipped technically, and of high
ideals, who accepted the Revolution and trained the students of
the rising generation. These men were Glazunov, Steinberg,
Ippolitov-Ivanov, Myaskovsky and Glière, all except the last being
pupils of Rimsky-Korsakov—and even Glière, had absorbed the
Korsakov tradition at second-hand through Ippolitov-Ivanov.
Glazunov we know in this country by his charming ballet music
and his pleasantly lyrical but not particularly important symphon-

---

a flat; some years ago it spent two and a half million rubles on a Composers'
House in Moscow, with its own concert hall and library, as well as restaur-
ants, social rooms, and so on, where nearly 150 musicians can live with their
families in sound-proof apartments,

ies; he was unable to work with the Soviet authorities after a time and in 1926 joined the exiles. Of the other composers of this bridging group most of us know Ippolitov-Ivanov only by his *Caucasian Sketches*, Myaskovsky by some of his numerous symphonies—he reached his twenty-first in 1941 and has probably thrown off one or two more by this time—and Steinberg and Glière not at all. (Their most important works since the Revolution are the former's Fourth Symphony, *Turksib*, and the latter's ballet *Red Poppy* and opera *Shakh-Senem*.) But these men matter less for what they have written than for what they have taught. Of the outstanding Soviet composers of the present day, Shostakovich and Shaporin were pupils of Steinberg; Khachaturyan, Shebalin, Kabalevsky of Myaskovsky; the now almost forgotten Mosolov, of *Steel Foundry* notoriety, studied under both Myaskovsky and Glière. Each one of these composers is therefore artistically descended from Rimsky-Korsakov and in one way or another continues the Russian 'classical' tradition.

That tradition was most seriously assailed round about 1920–2, when the militant and triumphant proletariat set about the liquidation of all bourgeois art—and tended to regard the music of Tchaikovsky, Borodin and Rimsky-Korsakov as bourgeois. This was the period when even the established operatic classics such as *Carmen*, were enthusiastically provided with new libretti of the proper ideological tendency. During the more settled days of Lenin's New Economic Policy the tension was relaxed, iconoclasm was dropped, and writers and composers and painters were allowed almost, if not quite unlimited freedom; the new Soviet music was as advanced and experimental as the music that was being written in Western Europe at the same time. The 'NEP period', as it is called, was in some respects the golden age of Soviet music. It passed with the launching of the first Five Year Plan in 1929, in which writers and artists of every kind were expected to collaborate, and since then, although Government control of art and literature has sometimes been slightly relaxed, it has always been very effectively exercised. Since 1932, in particular, writers and artists have been given an official ideal epitomized in the phrase 'Soviet realism'. The aim of Soviet art must be not merely to reflect life but to give it direction; it must be (as I have said) proletarian, comprehensible to the masses, not merely to sophisticated connoisseurs; and it must not be pessimistic. But although 'Soviet realism' could be defined and practised in literature, its embodiment in music was much more problematic—so problematic that to this day nobody is absolutely sure what 'Soviet realism' in music really is] When Shostakovich's now famous—or notorious—opera, *The Lady Macbeth of the Mtsensk District*, was produced in 1934, it was hailed as a masterpiece of 'Soviet realism'; two years later it was officially denounced as a supreme example of the sophisticated 'formalism' that had flourished in the 1920's. But the ban on *The Lady Macbeth* at any rate cleared the air and showed the Soviet composer what model he was *not* to follow; at the same time the lyrical, folk-songish opera which Ivan Dzerzhinsky had based on Sholokhov's popular novel *Quiet Flows the Don* was held up to admiration and hailed as marking the opening of a new epoch in Soviet opera.

Since then, indeed even before then, the Soviet composer who has listened to 'advanced' modern music has done so at his peril, for if he gets any of its influences into his system the best thing he can do is to get them out again as quickly as possible; if he picks up more than a certain amount of harmonic spiciness he is liable to be accused of being a mere 'formalist', the most damaging thing you can call him. But the good Soviet composer does not want to listen to these not-very-sirenlike voices. Whether he is writing 'mass-songs' for the workers, and Red Army songs and marches, and songs for the youth organizations, or whether he is creating monumental choral symphonies and lyrical string quartets, he is producing music for the people, his people, the people of the U.S.S.R., music to entertain or inspire them if not actually for them to sing or play. It is likely to mean something to similar people outside the U.S.S.R., he thinks, but whether or not it interests the ordinary so-called 'musical publics' of other lands is no concern of his. Even from the material aspect of publication, the State Music Publishing house has probably been far more concerned with meeting the vast home demands on its production than with pushing its wares in foreign markets, except in so far as was necessary for propaganda purposes.

If the Russian musician before the war looked anywhere away from the job in hand, it was not westward to the 'bourgeois and capitalist' world but eastward to the native peoples of the Caucasian and Asiatic republics of the Soviet Union. Each of these autonomous races—the Uzbeks, the Tajiks, the Turkomans, the Armenians, the Bashkirs, and the rest—has its own folk-music, and the central government, like the local governments of the separate states, has followed an enlightened policy of encouraging all these native cultures and of not attempting to impose forms of 'Russian' culture from Moscow. These non-Russian peoples of the U.S.S.R. have their own national theatres; their outstanding executive artists—singers and actors and instrumentalists alike—are officially honoured just like Russian artists; their composers are encouraged to write operas on native themes (in both the musical and non-musical senses of the word). It is all part of the general policy of looking inward, of providing art for the people immediately at hand, art that is natural to them and that they can understand. But it has had this consequence, that Russian musicians, finding it inadvisable to look westward, have looked eastward and devoted a great deal of attention to study of the music of these Caucasian and Asiatic peoples. This study has resulted not only in a number of interesting analytical monographs but in a considerable quantity of music evolved from oriental musical idioms: such works as Shekhter's *Turkmenia* and Knipper's orchestral suites *Vanch* and *Stalinabad*. 'But is there anything new in that?' someone may be asking. 'Has not a certain amount of orientalism always been one of the most attractive ingredients of Russian music?' To which the reply is that the genuine orientalism of, say, *Vanch* differs from the pseudo-orientalism of *Scheherazade* as a Hebridean folk-song differs from Max Bruch's *Scottish Fantasia*. The orientalism of the Russian classics is either pure fake or the genuine article more or less conventionally Russified; the oriental essays of composers like Knipper and Shekhter and Khachaturyan are the fruit of their attempts to saturate themselves in Asiatic folk-music, in these cases the music of the Tajiks and Turkomans and Caucasians, and to evolve from it a higher type of musical organism playable by ordinary Western instruments or orchestras, yet otherwise free from the conventions of European music.

Next to this interest in the music of the non-Russian peoples of the U.S.S.R., the most characteristic product of contemporary

Russian music is a vast, epic type of symphony for chorus and orchestra, spiritually descended from Beethoven's Ninth, Berlioz's *Symphonie funèbre et triomphale* and the symphonies of Mahler (which enjoyed considerable popularity in Russia before the present war). These symphonies—Shaporin's, Knipper's *Far Eastern* and *Komsomol*, Shebalin's *Lenin*, Shostakovich's *Leningrad* and the rest of them—may not be better music than the dexterous productions of, say, Shostakovich in his earlier years, but they are much more truly representative of the ideals of Soviet music to-day. The epic, the heroic, the monumental: these are the highest aims of the good Soviet composer. If he feels them to be beyond him, he must content himself with being lyrical. Naturally, then, he is most successful if his own innate tendency is to the simple and melodious; 'clever' composers like Shostakovich and Knipper, composers who have been obliged to sit on their intellectual safety valves, are obviously rather ill at ease under these conditions. The most successful men are the Glières and Myaskovskys and Shaporins in the older generation, and the Shebalins and Kabalevskys and Dzerzhinskys in the younger—musicians who, as Richard Strauss is said to have remarked of himself when he was writing the *Alpine Symphony*, 'wish to give music as a cow gives milk'; when Shostakovich tries to do that, as in his Fifth Symphony and some of his more recent chamber music, he is liable to produce milk adulterated with chalk and water.

Fortunately or unfortunately, so many of us in this country have lost our taste for milk; like Nebuchadnezzar's diet of grass, 'it may be wholesome, but it is not good'. We are accustomed to stronger liquors and we generally find Soviet music most palatable when the composer has contrived to drop in a spot of vodka on the sly. Which is a pity. Not (I think) because we have debased our tastes and ruined our palates, but because our distaste for musical milk is a hindrance to our appreciation of the music of a people whose culture it is most important that we should understand.

II. DMITRY SHOSTAKOVICH

BY MORE or less general consent, Dmitry Shostakovich (born at St. Petersburg in 1906), is acknowledged to be the most significant composer yet produced by the Soviet Union. Like a good many other generally acknowledged truths, that judgment is open to challenge. Despite the great nervous vitality of his best work and despite his equally great technical dexterity, it is arguable that his reputation really rests on little more substantial than the brilliant First Symphony, which first drew the world's attention to him sixteen years ago, and that equally brilliant but remarkably unequal opera, *The Lady Macbeth of the Mtsensk District*. But my main purpose here is less to attempt a general revaluation of Shostakovich's work than to show how the career of an undeniably gifted, even if somewhat overrated, musician has been affected by those changing art-politics I have just outlined and which I must now describe in more detail. By showing his work against this background, which has a trick of occasionally becoming the foreground, one should be able to see both in better perspective.

When Shostakovich wrote that F minor Symphony, his Op.10, in 1925 while still a student at the Leningrad Conservatoire, the Soviet Union was in the middle of the NEP period. After passing through the *Sturm und Drang* of the actual Revolution and the ensuing Civil War, political events that were reflected artistically in Futurism and 'Proletkult' (i.e. proletarian culture, actively hostile to bourgeois culture), Russia reach a sort of convalescent stage, a stage not only of relative economic, but of relative artistic, freedom. In literature the 'fellow-travellers', as Trotsky called them, the non-Communist writers who more or less accepted the Revolution, were tolerated. Even Formalism, begotten of Russian Futurism, the doctrine that literature is 'an evolution of literary forms and genres', that it is 'primarily an art', and that 'literary science and literary criticism must in the first place deal with the specific *devices* of that art and not with its philosophical, social, psychological or biological contents'[1]—even this very un-Russian

[1] Gleb Struve: *Soviet Russian Literature*: Routledge 1935.

view of art was allowed to exist as a variety of non-Communist literature, though Trotsky and other Marxist critics considered it 'one of the worst expressions of the bourgeois spirit'. This period of toleration opened about 1921–2, and in 1925, the very year of the Shostakovich Symphony, still greater freedom was granted by a resolution of the Central Committee of the Communist Party.

Shostakovich's First Symphony, then, was composed in surroundings that did not differ essentially from those of a young Western composer at the same period. (The Leningrad of Shostakovich's youth heard productions of Schreker's *Der ferne Klang*, of Křenek's *Jonny* and *Der Sprung über den Schatten*, of *Petrushka*, *Pulcinella* and *Wozzeck*; Hindemith was a welcome visitor there.) The Symphony is 'pure' music and it is 'modern' music (modern harmonically, and in its transparency of texture and freedom from romanticism). It is a mixture of styles—from Tchaikovsky in the second subject of the first movement:

Ex. 1

to Prokofiev in the second movement and the first *allegro molto* theme of the finale:

Ex. 2

But that was only to be expected of a work which, as the composer has told us, 'was my thesis for my final examination at the

Conservatoire'. And running through the Symphony are a number
of traits that we can now recognize as characteristic of Shostakovich: the mosaic nature of the thematic conception (almost remini-
scent of the mid eighteenth-century *galant* style), the rather dry,
almost Hindemithian 'motor' energy that often takes the place of
logical sequence, the cut of the opening trumpet theme:

Ex.3

which may be compared with the similar brass-theme near the
beginning of the Third Symphony:

Ex. 4

the hopping bassoon theme that answers it (a type of theme that
runs through much of Shostakovich's work from the·first of the
Three Fantastic Dances for piano, Op.1, through the first subject[1]
of the *Allegro non troppo* of this same Symphony:

Ex. 5

[1] From which, I need hardly point out, Ex. 2 is derived and which is
already adumbrated in Ex. 3.

to the scherzo of the Fifth Symphony), the extraordinary pre-
dilection for long and important wood-wind solos, the use of
the piano as an orchestral instrument, the Rimsky-Korsakov-like
treatment of the percussion (even as a 'solo' group uncovered
by other instruments). As a whole, and in some details, the Symphony reminds one of the First Symphony of Tchaikovsky; it
promised the advent of a composer of Tchaikovsky's stature. But
that promise has not been fulfilled. Why? I put forward two ex-
planations. One, the political background of Shostakovich's later
work, will emerge gradually; the other can be put more concisely
in the words of a statement by Shostakovich's composition professor, Maximilian Steinberg, at the time of the *Lady Macbeth*
scandal:[1]

'A number of speakers have referred to Shostakovich's First
Symphony as one of his best works, but no one has reminded us
that this Symphony was written in the Conservatoire class. The
First Symphony, the highest possible expression of his talent, is
the result of his study in the Conservatoire. I was very distressed by
Shostakovich's published allegation that in the Conservatoire we
only "hindered him from composing".'

The fairly obvious inference is that Steinberg himself had had
some hand in the polishing of the Symphony, that his relationship
to it was (shall we say?) similar to Stanford's rumoured relationship
to *Hiawatha's Wedding Feast*. That may be one reason why
Shostakovich has never done anything as good as his Op.10.
Steinberg continued:

'On leaving the Conservatoire, Shostakovich came under the
influence of people who professed the musical principles of the
"extremist" West. This was in 1925. . . . One of Shostakovich's
first compositions was his sonata, written in contemporary idiom
and called by him *October Symphony*. Already in this there was
an unhealthy tendency to "adapt" formalistic language for the
expression of revolutionary ideas. The most extreme statement of
Shostakovich's "new" tendency was the *Aphorisms*. When he
brought them to me, I told him that I understood nothing in them,
that they were quite foreign—after which he ceased coming to me.'

[1] At a meeting of the Leningrad Union of Soviet Composers, reported in
Sovetskaya Muzika, May 1936.

The truth of these remarks is fully attested by the compositions of the next period—the Prelude and Scherzo for string octet, Op.11, the Piano Sonata, Op.12 (1926), the ten *Aphorisms* for piano, Op.13 (1927), the Second Symphony ('Symphonic Dedication to October') (1927), the opera based on Gogol's *The Nose* (1928–9), and the Third Symphony ('First of May') (1929)—though they are at variance with a statement made by Shostakovich himself some years later:[1]

'[On leaving the Conservatoire] I suddenly realized that music is not only a combination of sounds arranged in this melody or that, but an art which is capable of expressing the most varied ideas and feelings by means of its specific qualities. I did not easily win through to this conviction. It is sufficient to say that during the whole of 1926 I did not write a single note.'[2]

This, of course, is simply an attempt to clear himself of the charge of 'formalism'. But the musical facts are against him. The pieces for string octet bubble over with technical exuberance; the Piano Sonata was written under the influences of early Prokofiev (already evident in the *Three Fantastic Dances* and the Symphony), Stravinksy and Hindemith; and the *Aphorisms* are still more Stravinskyan. I do not know the Second Symphony, but *The Nose* is full of grotesque and satirical music—as the subject demands. It is all very flippant and piquant and rather vulgar; the parodies (e.g. of Italian cantilena and coloratura) are amusing:

Ex. 6

('*What do you say? Explain yourself*')

[1] Quoted by Kurt London in *The Seven Soviet Arts*, Faber, 1937.
[2] Despite this statement, I give this date to the Piano Sonata on the authority of M. Druskin (article 'On the Piano Music of D. Shostakovich' in *Sovetskaya Muzika*, November 1935).

but though one detects in the vulgarity the composer's consciousness of a proletarian audience, the music is essentially 'clever' and
sophisticated.

Up to this point, however, Shostakovich had developed freely
and naturally, though one may deplore his superficiality, his sedu-
lous aping, his general failure to fulfil the promise of his First
Symphony. But he had followed his own line, even though it was
a descending line and not a very individual one. One cannot say
that quite so certainly of his next big work, the *First of May*
Symphony, Op.20 (1929).[1] This is certainly a much poorer work
than the First Symphony, but it is not without points of interest.
Like the Second (by all accounts), it consists of a single connected
movement though one can easily trace the remains of the traditional first movement, slow movement, scherzo and finale, the last
consisting of a choral setting of some verses 'On the First of May'
by a poet who has wisely concealed his identity. The Symphony
opens with a clarinet solo apparently intended to suggest a spring
morning and the rest of the work appears to be programme music
of a rather naïve type. It used to be held against the post-Wagner-
ians that they were rhetorical; Shostakovich in this Symphony is
mob-oratorical, with trombone-recitatives, long horn-and-trumpet
duets accompanied only by the side-drum, and hysterical melodic
passages for the entire orchestra *unisono*. Granted that a certain
amount of the actual musical material, particularly the bustling
filling-in, is recognizably Shostakovich's, as well as the obvious
rhythms mercilessly reiterated and the rowdy orchestration (with
xylophone well to the fore) and that anything like musical logic is
much rarer even than in the First Symphony, one cannot help
feeling that the composer is playing a part. He is by nature a wit
(or a humorist), and wits do not make good hymn writers. He tries
to be Marxian, but fantastic Gogolian humour keeps breaking in.
A stranger hotch-potch of commonplace, bad taste and misdirected
cleverness has never been called a symphony.

But the most significant thing about the Third Symphony is its

[1] Nor possibly of its predecessor, the 'Dedication to October', which is
said to begin with a suggestion of chaos and anarchy and to proceed, by way
of trumpet calls, instrumental and vocal recitatives, and other more or less
realistic devices, to the building up of a massive and triumphant conclusion
in which the orchestra is reinforced by a chorus.

date, for, it will be remembered, 1929 was an important turning
point in Soviet history. The NEP period ended and the first Five
Year Plan was launched, with serious consequences for all creative
artists in the Soviet Union. Under the Plan they lost the freedom
they had enjoyed during the last seven years; they were told that
art had 'social tasks'; Formalism, never popular, became absolutely
taboo. Proletkult celebrated its triumph and literary 'shock
brigades' were formed to see that authors kept to the 'strict Party
line'; indeed, the 'proletarians' went to such lengths, and with such
dismal results in the field of literature, that in 1932 they had to be
sharply checked, their intolerant groups and associations were dis-
solved, and for two or three years there was a slight relaxation of
official pressure on writers and artists. Although music was by its
nature obviously less exposed to the winds of Party policy than
literature or painting, it by no means remained unaffected. So we
find the one-time Formalist, Mosolov, writing his *Steel Foundry*.
And Shostakovich, too, whose early works were also decidedly
Formalistic, composed first this *First of May* Symphony and then,
all in the period 1929–32, two ballets, *The Golden Age*, Op.22
(produced in 1931), and *The Bolt*, of which the former is strongly
anti-Fascist and the latter on an industrial theme, and an opera,
The Lady Macbeth of the Mtsensk District, Op.29 (produced in
1934) which is strongly anti-bourgeois. The theme of *The Golden
Age*—I know nothing about *The Bolt*—is the clash between Fascist
and Soviet visitors to 'The Golden Age', an industrial exhibition
in a great capitalist city; the Fascists include a cabaret star, the
Russians a Soviet football team with a lady supporter (a member
of the League of Young Communists) and the wicked behaviour of
the bourgeois police would be quite incredible if we did not know
what the Gestapo is capable of doing.[1] Of the music I know only
the orchestral suite of four numbers (Introduction, Adagio, Polka,
and Dance), but one can gather from this at least a general idea
of Shostakovich's musical approach to the subject. In the music
associated with the Fascists and the police and the bourgeois he
generally further exploits that vulgar, grotesque, satirical vein he
had opened up in *The Nose*; thus the polka in Act III, with its

[1] The action is described at length in Cyril W. Beaumont's *Complete
Book of Ballets* (Putnam, 1937).

flippant xylophoning, is called 'Once upon a time in Geneva' and accompanies a choreographic skit on the League of Nations. In this way, by association, the musical methods which in *The Nose* merely underlined and exaggerated Gogol's fantastic humour are here given a political sense.

Similar methods are employed in *The Lady Macbeth of the Mtsensk District*. They are not used alone; indeed the opera is an even more remarkable hotchpotch of styles than most of Shostakovich's scores. There is a good deal of serious music in the work. That associated with Katerina, this provincial Russian 'Lady Macbeth' of the eighteen-forties, is lyrical, even sentimental, e.g. her song in Scene 3, 'Once from the window I saw a little nest under the roof':

Ex.7

The music of the opening scene evokes the aimless monotony of her life, 'the dullness, the Russian dullness, the dullness of a merchant's house which they say makes it quite a pleasure to strangle oneself', as Leskov put it in the story on which the opera is based. Some of it has a vivid, almost pantomimic quality in the direct line of descent from Dargomïzhsky and Mussorgsky, and there are pantomimic elements in the notorious love music, too. The song of the old convict at the beginning of the last act, the chorus of convicts, and the final dying away of this chorus at the end, after Katerina's murder of her rival and her suicide, are genuinely beautiful. The great passacaglia entr'acte connecting the two scenes of Act II (the discovery of Katerina's affair with the clerk, Sergey, his flogging by her father-in-law, and the murder of the father-in-law—and Katerina's beating by her husband and *his* murder) is extraordinarily powerful in its conveying of a sense of oppression by an inescapable destiny:

Ex. 8

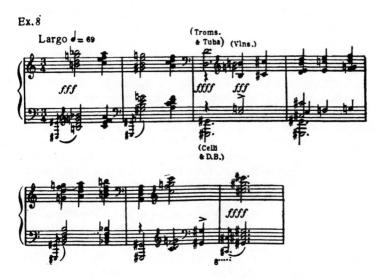

It is one of the best things Shostakovich has ever written. But there is also an enormous amount of parody, of rather cheap cleverness in the music. The characterization (and caricaturing) of the lecherous and sadistic father-in-law is genuinely clever and is kept in focus, but Sergey's frivolity and general worthlessness are suggested by frivolous, worthless music—suggestive of operetta or even the music hall—which is right out of focus. The policemen in the Third Act inform us that their lot is not a happy one to music that is less pure comic opera than burlesque of comic opera; the bridal song in the following scene is a burlesque of Russian folk-song opera of the Rimsky-Korsakov variety. There was no hint of these farcical elements in Leskov's story; he has told it with ironic detachment[1] like the fine artist he was. Shostakovich and his collaborator in the

[1] English translation in *The Sentry, and Other Stories* by Leskov. (John Lane, 1922.)

libretto (A. Préys) have not only altered all the values and all the characters—whitewashing Katerina's as far as possible, and blackening everyone else's—but turned the whole thing into a grotesque satire on the old Russian 'merchant class', with a subsidiary attack on the old police gratuitously thrown in. Even Sergey the underdog, who is at first not altogether bad in Leskov, is made the completely despicable symbol of a class hateful to good Communists: 'through Sergey's handsome, gallant exterior peers the future *kulak*', the composer explained. But the important point is that the frivolous, parodic elements in the music, the elements that are 'out of focus', are all closely connected with these politically-motivated alterations. It is not easy, indeed it is not possible, to draw clear lines dividing the element of pure Leskov in the opera from the distortions and additions of the librettists, or between the serious music (whether lyrical, or pantomimic in a post-Mussorgskian manner) and the worthless; but in so far as one can, the two lines tend to coincide.

In the period between the completion of *Lady Macbeth* in 1932 and its immensely successful production in Moscow on 22 January 1934, Shostakovich produced a group of works including the Twenty-Four Preludes, Op.34 and the Piano Concerto, Op.35. Close on their heels came the 'Cello Sonata, Op.40 (1934), a ballet *The Clear Stream* (1935) and a Fourth Symphony (1936), which for reasons that will be discussed later was never performed. Although he was now nearly thirty, these compositions show the same diversity of styles as his earliest works; the diversity is in fact more marked than ever. Soviet critics have discovered in the Preludes reminiscences of Prokofiev, Richard Strauss, Chopin and Tchaikovsky, in the 'Cello Sonata of Borodin, Liszt, Prokofiev, Beethoven and Mozart. The Piano Concerto—with its curiously constituted orchestra of strings and solo trumpet—is now fairly familiar to Western listeners, and that too consists of 'many-coloured silken patches sewn on a coarse peasant's coat' (to borrow an image from the nineteenth-century novelist Grigorovich); it begins seriously with one of those oddly straggling melodies into which Shostakovich tends to lapse when he writes lyrically:

Ex.9

but lapses with the second subject into a sort of can-can. The composer's deliberate banality, his delight in shocking us, reach their apogee in the finale, which suggests a parody on Offenbach by Prokofiev—when it does not suggest a cornet player performing outside a public-house. It is funny, but it is incredibly vulgar. The 'Cello Sonata is a much better work; its first three movements, particularly the scherzo and slow movement, are among the best things Shostakovich has done. (The element of parody reappears in the finale.) Of the music of *The Clear Stream*, the action of which takes place on a collective farm,[1] the farm that gives its name to the ballet, I know nothing—except that its modernity involved it in the *Lady Macbeth* catastrophe.

In emphasizing Shostakovich's stylistic patchiness, one must not lose sight of the fact that he *has* a style, that this very eclecticism—this *sort* of eclecticism—is itself peculiar to Shostakovich, apart from a number of traits that are personal in the more usual sense. Despite its obvious echoes, the music is always easily recognizable as *his*. The reminiscences are not undigested or half digested 'influences'; they are rather in the nature of sarcastic allusions even when they are not directly parodic. But a severe check was soon to be put to Shostakovich's parody and sarcasm, his vulgarity and his modernism.

In 1932 at the same time that the Soviet Government temporarily relaxed its pressure on writers and artists to some extent, it gave them the slogan mentioned in the previous chapter, 'socialist realism', a slogan coined, it is said, by Stalin himself. They were free to create as they liked, *within the limits of 'socialist realism'*. The

[1] See Beaumont's *Complete Book of Ballets*.

only difficulty was to define 'socialist realism'. To quote a literary authority:[1]

'In interpreting the meaning of this newest catchword the leading Soviet literary commentators seem to admit that it must be taken in a rather broad sense, and that it includes a great variety of styles. But in their theoretical disquisitions they fail to define it more or less precisely even as a broadly understood method, and when it comes to its practical manifestations the position becomes still more confused.'

'Inasmuch as the stress in this latest literary formula is laid on the word "Realism", its point is directed against certain formalistic and stylistic innovations which tend to subordinate the description of real life and living men to formal and stylistic designs.'

Socialist realism 'is fundamentally optimistic, it says "yes" to life, while the pre-revolutionary bourgeois Realism was fundamentally pessimistic and often led to a morbid and unhealthy attitude to the world. Drawing the antithesis a little further, we may come to the conclusion (though this conclusion is not to be found in the discourses of the Communist critics) that Socialist realism is potentially conservative, and in doing so we should not be wide off the mark.'[2]

'There are . . . partisans of Socialist Realism who insist that it must look out for *heroes*, that it must reflect the *heroic* features of the great revolutionary epoch.'

'The statutes of the Union of Soviet Writers stipulate that Socialist Realism must tend not only to describe the realities of the new world, but also to *reform* men, to educate them towards Socialism.'

If the practical manifestation of socialist realism was a matter of confusion in literature, it was still more so in music. Not only in pure music, but in opera and ballet. To this day no one has satisfactorily defined what socialist realism amounts to in, say, a sym-

---

[1] Gleb Struve: op. cit.

[2] Artists who took a more liberal view of socialist realism soon got into trouble. 'Realism as we knew it once is merely actual, that is static,' Alexander Tayrov, the theatrical producer, told Kurt London. 'Socialist realism, on the other hand, is actual and future, and so dynamic. Now, just as each artist sees the future with his own eyes, socialist realism can show the future in the most varied ways.' But his liberal interpretation of the formula soon resulted in his dismissal.

phony or a string quartet, though clearness of texture, melodious-
ness, general comprehensibility, optimism, the monumental,
heroism and patriotism are all considered desirable (the first four,
indispensable) qualities; socialist realism is above all the antithesis
of formalism, of music for music's sake. When music is mated with
words or dramatic action, of course, the problem is a little simpler;
yet so little was socialist realism understood at first that *The Lady
Macbeth of Mtsensk* was accepted as an embodiment of it. Ostretsov,
a critic whose political orthodoxy was irreproachable, while deplor-
ing such dramatic points as the attempt to make Katerina a sympathetic figure and such musical ones as the formalist and modernist
tendencies in the chorus of workmen in Act I and the entr'actes
leading to the third and eighth scenes, still concluded that the opera
'could have been written only by a Soviet composer brought up in
the best traditions of Soviet culture and actively fighting by means
of his art for the victory of the new social *Weltanschauung*. In its
serious artistic worth and high level of musical mastery . . . the
opera is the result of the general success of socialist construction,
of the correct policy of the Party towards all sections of the country's
cultural life, and of the deep significance of that new upwelling of
creative strength evoked on the musical front by the historic decree
of the Central Committee of the All-Union Communist Party of
23 April 1932.'

The blow fell in January 1936. On 28 January—eleven days after
Stalin and Molotov had, in circumstances of considerable publicity,
expressed their approval of Dzerzhinsky's *Quiet Flows the Don*, a
work of a very different type and quality—*Pravda* appeared with
a now historic article 'Muddle instead of Music', which asserted
that:

'from the first minute the listener to *The Lady Macbeth* is dumb-
founded by a deliberately discordant, confused stream of sounds.
Fragments of melody, embryonic phrases appear—only to disappear again in the din, the grinding and the screaming. To follow
this "music" is difficult, to remember it impossible. So it goes on
almost through the opera. Cries take the place of song. If by chance
the composer lapses into simple, comprehensible melody, he is
scared at such a misfortune and quickly plunges into confusion
again. . . . All this arises not from the composer's lack of talent,

but from his not knowing how to express strong and simple feelings. This is music deliberately "taken by the scruff of the neck" so that nothing reminds you of classical opera music, so that it has nothing in common with symphonic sound, with simple, popular musical speech. . . . It is Leftist[1] confusion instead of natural, human music. . . . The composer has evidently never asked himself what a Soviet audience expects in music. He has written music in code, so disguising it that it can appeal only to aesthete-formalists who have lost all healthy taste.'

The article also denounced the 'coarse, primitive, vulgar' naturalism of the action. On 6 February appeared a second article, 'Falsity in Ballet', attacking *The Clear Stream*:

'According to the libretto the action takes place on a collective farm in the Kuban. But actually there is neither Kuban nor collective farm, but tinsel *paysans* from a pre-Revolutionary chocolate box who depict "joy" in dances that have nothing in common with the folk dances of the Kuban or anywhere else. . . . Shostakovich's music exactly suits the ballet. It is true there are fewer tricks, fewer strange and barbarous harmonies than in *The Lady Macbeth of the Mtsensk District*. The music of the ballet is simpler but it has nothing whatever to do with collective farms or the Kuban. The composer has adopted the same contemptuous attitude to the folk-songs of the Kuban as the librettists and choreographers have done to its folk dances. So the music is characterless. It strums away and expresses nothing. We learn from the programme that it was partly transferred from the miscarried "industrial" ballet *The Bolt*. It is clear what happens when the same music has to express different scenes. Actually it expressed only the composer's indifference to his subject.'

This official denunciation, endorsed in 'constructive discussions' by Shostakovich's colleagues of the Union of Soviet Composers, had the crushing effect one would expect. The composer completed his Fourth Symphony but withdrew it while in rehearsal as 'not in accordance with his new creative principles'. But he was not crushed for long. To quote Georgy Khubov:[2]

[1] Western readers unfamiliar with Soviet terminology may be amused to know that for some years 'Leftist' has been a term of abuse in the U.S.S.R.
[2] Article on the Fifth Symphony in *Sovetskaya Muzika*, March 1938.

'Shostakovich took the just criticism of his formalistic errors very seriously. For two years he worked stubbornly and intensively at a new creative development of his gifts. . . . Recognizing the impossibility of any such growth unless he decidedly and categorically abandoned his formalistic position, and beautifully understanding the danger and falsity of a facile, superficial "rebuilding", Shostakovich chose the line of greatest resistance, the only true line: of fundamental, organic overcoming of his formalistic errors by an intense internal struggle. The result of this great labour was the Fifth Symphony, which the author himself has described as "a Soviet artist's practical creative reply to just criticism".'

As Khubov puts it, this Fifth Symphony is Shostakovich's 'first appearance as an avowed artist-realist', his 'first serious attempt to grapple with ideas of a philosophical order', and his 'first address to a broad audience, and not to a narrow circle of *melomanes*, in clear, simple and expressive language'. The 'philosophical idea' underlying this Fifth Symphony, Op.47 (1938), is more or less frankly autobiographical. 'The theme of my symphony', Shostakovich tells us:[1]

'is the stabilization of a personality. In the centre of this composition—conceived lyrically from beginning to end—I saw a man with all his experiences. The finale resolves the tragically tense impulses of the earlier movements into optimism and joy of living.'

Accordingly, Russian commentators see the first movement as a Faust-like struggle, full of self-questionings but also of memories of childhood and youth; the second as 'an ironic smile over the irrevocable past'; the third as filled with tragic renunciation, with 'tears and suffering' (one is glad to have the composer's own assurance that 'I wrote the third movement in three days'). And the composer himself tells us that 'the finale answers all the questions asked in the previous movements', though the most sympathetic listeners, Russian and foreign alike, nearly all agree in finding it (particularly the D major coda) rather unconvincing. But to what does it all amount musically? Not, surely, to very much. The second movement, which comes most dangerously near to the old grotesque, malicious Shostakovich (and has had to have its mildly parodic element explained away as of quite a different type from the

[1] Article in *Vechernyaya Moskva*, 25 January 1938.

old), is merely tame; the harmonic banality has extracted any possible sting. The slow movement—also a little suspect in orthodox Communist circles on grounds of 'subjective sentimentalism'— merely confirms one's suspicion that Shostakovich cannot write even a moderately good tune:

Ex.10

And the first movement, evolved from poor, dry material:

Ex.11

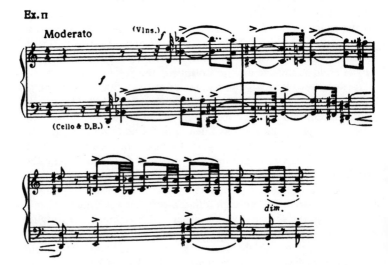

shows no distinction of symphonic thought. Stylistically, however, the Symphony does show greater homogeneity than anything earlier by Shostakovich known to me, though even here the homogeneity is by no means complete. One notices the old predilections for straggling themes, string *glissandi*, wind solos, and brutally reiterated rhythms, for the xylophone and for the piano (treated rather as a xylophone with greater resources). It is all recognizable as Shostakovich; but it is Shostakovich exorcised—and he was certainly much livelier in the days when the devil possessed him. The devil caused some repellant antics but he never allowed his victim to be merely dull.

Since the Fifth Symphony, Shostakovich has produced a String Quartet, Op.49 (1938), a Sixth Symphony, Op.53 (1939), an operetta, *The Twelve Chairs* (1940), based on the humorous story of the same name[1] by Ilya Ilf and Eugeny Petrov, a Piano Quintet (1941), and a Seventh Symphony, Op.60 (1942), the much heralded *Leningrad* Symphony. Somewhere in the background, too, there is another symphony, a *Lenin* Symphony; No. 6 was said to be inspired by Mayakovsky's poem, 'Vladimir Ilich Lenin', but there is no hint of this on the score; then, early in 1940, it was announced that Shostakovich was working on a 'seventh symphony' for orchestra, chorus and soloist, with words drawn from the same Mayakovsky poem, but apparently the composition was interrupted by the German invasion and the consequent work on the intensely patriotic *Leningrad* Symphony.

Of the four instrumental works—I know nothing of *The Twelve Chairs*—the best is the Quartet, of which the viola theme of the slow movement:

Ex. 12

[1] The English translation (Methuen, 1930) is called *Diamonds to Sit On*. The book deals with some earlier adventures of Ostap Bender, the rascally hero of their better-known *Golden Calf*.

nearly dispels my suspicion that Shostakovich cannot write even a moderately good tune. (It does not quite dispel it.) Although composed under the immediate shadow of the Fifth Symphony, it is a more attractive work: mainly lyrical, with just enough tang of modernism to give it savour and to make Soviet critics regard it with some suspicion. The colourless finale, reminding one of the dry bones of late eighteenth-century classicism, anticipates the style of the suite-like Piano Quintet. The most striking feature of the Sixth Symphony is its slow, elegiac first movement; the *allegro* second movement and the vulgar galop finale both tend dangerously to revert to Shostakovich's earlier manner, though in an emasculated form. The prevailing diatonicism is apt to run off the rails, but Shostakovich does get a certain piquancy from unexpected juxtapositions of keys (a favourite trick of Prokofiev's). The scoring—with the inevitable xylophone, and wood-wind and percussion solos—suggests that Shostakovich has learned nothing and forgotten nothing.

The Seventh Symphony, 'dedicated to the ordinary Soviet citizens who have become the heroes of the present war', has been described as:

'A patriotic call to arms, with the wrathful spirit of denunciation characteristic of an anti-Fascist document. Two worlds are opposed to one another in the Symphony. One is a world of thought and feeling, of great passions and noble aspirations. It appears in the very first theme. . . . It comes again at the end of the exposition, and it appears once more in the recapitulation of the first movement, where the same music becomes a requiem for those who have laid down their lives for the freedom of their country. The other world is brutal, senseless and implacable. Against the background of constant drumming there are sounds of a martial theme. It is repeated twelve times, not developing, only growing in volume. It advances, yet there is something static about it. Cruel like the mechanism of force, this music arouses a feeling of hatred, it calls for vengeance. It contains nothing naturalistic, no "war sounds". It is a psychological portrait of the enemy, ruthless and denouncing.'

The composer himself has described the rest of the work:

'The second movement, the scherzo, is a rather elaborate lyrical episode. It brings back pleasant memories of happy days. There is a hint of wistful sadness about the entire movement. The third movement, a hymn to life, a paean to nature, merges into the fourth without a pause. Like the first movement, the fourth is fundamental to this composition. The first movement symbolizes struggle, the fourth heralds approaching victory. The fourth movement begins with a brief bravura introduction which echoes the central episode of the third movement. The second theme of the fourth movement is triumphant. It is the summit of the whole symphony. After a calm, confident development, the theme evolves into its solemn and triumphant climax.'

Unfortunately the naïve programmatic elements in this Symphony are no more successful than those in the Third; for instance, the 'martial theme' of the first movement:

Ex. 13

'repeated twelve times, not developing, only growing in volume', certainly 'arouses a feeling of hatred'—if that is not too strong a word—but not against the Nazis. It would be difficult to imagine a greater contrast between this vast, turgidly scored work, Mahlerian in conception and (to some extent) in details of execution, and the clear, concise First Symphony; it is hardly an exaggeration to say that their only point in common is the treatment of the percussion. And whether we consider the Seventh Symphony the result of the composer's natural evolution or the consequence of the circumstances in which he wrote it, it is equally disappointing. To say that is not to condemn the Symphony for not being what Shostakovich never intended it to be. It is an essay in a symphonic genre—the vast and monumental and heroic—much cultivated in the Russia that has taken 'socialist realism' as its artistic watchword. Other Soviet composers have cultivated it with some success and one studies their efforts with interest and sympathy, but it is a most unsuitable medium for a composer of Shostakovich's natural tendencies. Whether the blame for attempting it rests on him or on circumstances one cannot venture to say.

III. SERGEY PROKOFIEV

THE EXTERNAL circumstances of a composer's life do not often have much bearing on the creative periods of his career. Life—in this superficial sense—is one thing, art another, and the symphonies a man writes before he marries or settles across the Atlantic are no different from those he has written before; or if they are different, they are not different *because* of this outward circumstance. But considering the special conditions of musical life in the U.S.S.R., there is some justification for drawing a distinction between the Prokofiev who lived in Germany and Paris and the U.S.A., and the Prokofiev who composes as a Soviet citizen. There is a remarkable difference between the Prokofiev of *The Buffoon* and *The Love for Three Oranges* and the steely glittering early piano concertos, and the Prokofiev of *Romeo and Juliet* and *Alexander Nevsky*, and one's first thought is to question whether the difference is entirely natural or whether it was influenced by the fact that in 1934 or 1935, after one or two short visits to the U.S.S.R., Prokofiev decided to settle once again in his native country, from which he had fled seventeen years before. We tend to think of Prokofiev as essentially an *enfant terrible*, a master of those veins of sarcasm, caricature and grotesqueness which run through so much Russian literature from Gogol onward and which are evidently very characterisic of the Russian intellect; the works he has written under the Hammer and Sickle show him as well behaved as Petya in his own *Petya and the Wolf* (who only annoyed Grandpa by going in the meadow) and not nearly as ingenious. It is natural to jump to the conclusion that this lyricism and simplicity are *voulus*. But why should Prokofiev, who was continuing a brilliant career outside Russia, have voluntarily returned to a land where he knew certain limitations would be imposed on his work, unless he felt that these limitations would be unimportant? The truth is, I think, that he had already been tending in this direction for some time—it is quite marked in the ballets *The Prodigal Son* (1928) and *On the Banks of the Borysthenes* (1930)—indeed, that this simplicity had always been an essential part of his make-up. The popular Classical Symphony of 1917 is not parodic, as has often been suggested. (People listened to it not as it was, but through the prisms of *The Buffoon* and the *Scythian Suite,* and took it for a *jeu d'esprit.*) Or consider Nos. 1, 8, and 9 of the *Visions fugitives* for piano, written during 1915–17. And I hope to show in a moment that the differences between the D major Violin Concerto begun in 1913, though not completed till 1921, and the G minor Violin Concerto of 1935 are no more than one would expect to find between any two works by the same composer separated by fourteen years. On the other hand there are signs, here and there, of a certain regretful longing for the cakes and ale.

Prokofiev did not actually become a Soviet citizen till about 1935, the year of the second violin concerto, but he had already been drawn into the Soviet orbit a year or two before and for critical purposes his work as a 'Soviet composer' may be said to begin with the *Symphonic Song* for orchestra, Op.57, written in 1933. The Supplementary Volume of *Grove* gives a list of his compositions up to 1937, ending with the *Songs of Our Days* for chorus and orchestra, Op.77; all the works with opus-numbers between these two are therefore Soviet works, and the list has since been extended by two cantatas for chorus and orchestra—*Alexander Nevsky* (based on music originally written for the Eisenstein film) and *Greeting to Stalin* (both 1939)—and two operas—*Simeon Kotko* (1941) and *War and Peace* (1942), the latter founded on Tolstoy's masterpiece—as well as by a sixth Piano Sonata (1940) and some minor compositions. To discuss all this corpus of work in a short essay is manifestly impossible; moreover a number of the scores are not available in this country; but the G minor Violin Concerto, *Romeo and Juliet* (1935), *Petya and the Wolf* (1936) and *Alexander Nevsky* (1939) provide a fairly adequate basis for discussion.

First, however, it may be worth while to glance at Prokofiev in the role of his own 'prodigal son', to see his work through the eyes of a well-known Soviet critic (A. Ostretsov) giving[1] his impression of the Moscow concert of 14 April 1934, when the *Symphonic Song* was played for the first time together with the first Piano Concerto and a suite of *Portraits* from the opera *The Gambler.* The new *Symphonic Song* did not please Ostretsov at all; he found it 'an extraordinarily symptomatic production, clearly revealing the tendencies of urbanized lyricism. The general effect is of weariness

C   [1] In *Sovetskaya Muzika,* June 1934.

and morbid resignation. The very material of the music is so abstract in idiom that vital and solid form is sometimes reduced to disembodied, half-real, melancholy arabesque. The composer uses his instrumental palette, charged with pallid autumnal colours, to create a series of instrumental pictures giving the impression of a gloomy elegiac background against which are heard—solitarily and, as it were, losing themselves in sonorous space—the melodies of solo instruments and dim complexes of separate instrumental groups. Emotionally the *Symphonic Song* is an elegy of solitude; its lyrical pathos is the pathos of the social and cultural dereliction of a man disillusioned with the present, unable to defend the past and unable to believe in the future. It re-echoes with the moods of the disillusioned and weary art of the urbanized lyricists of the contemporary West.

'We do not dispute Prokofiev's right to reflect the emotional world of "superfluous people" in the West, whose inward desolation imposes its inevitable stamp of rottenness and putrefaction on everything around it. But we do not share the composer's humanistic sympathy with these persons, a sympathy which gives his work a character not of satire but of intimate, lyrical community of feeling and experience. To mirror aright the anaemic "superfluous man" of the contemporary West, one must go some distance away from him—the distance of the Soviet witness watching the downfall of a dying class.

'The composer has called his work a song. Lyricism of the graveyard—that is the lot of the bourgeois artist, doomed sooner or later to be a musical priest, burying his dead and singing their requiem. And whoever speaks here of *song* is mistaken. The word "song" is, for the Soviet composer, always connected with the people he sees doing lively, joyous, full-blooded, valuable work in the shops and fields, with people going about their inconspicuous but important and necessary business. The singing quality is what makes a composition approachable by and comprehensible to the broad masses of our audiences. Prokofiev's *Symphonic Song* does not possess this quality; it is not a song in our sense of the word. We hear it as a symphonic monologue for the few, as a sad story of the decline of the overblown culture of individualism, to whose groans the composer pours out his sympathy, his fruitless, humanistic regrets and perhaps his quiet tears of compassion.'

In curious contrast with this denunciation was the praise, though much qualified praise, that Ostretsov gave the first Piano Concerto of 1911, which at any rate 'is characteristic of that side of the composer's art which impresses one by its optimism, by the energy of its creative exploration'. It represents 'an outgrown stage of development'; it was a fallacy of 'the ideologists of ASM'[1] to believe that the music of the Revolution could ever develop along these lines; Prokofiev's 'musical constructivism' was 'organically connected with narrow bourgeois subjectivism' and even 'snobbism'; but all the same, considered historically, this sort of art 'was in its time directed against routine, scholasticism, academicism and the stagnant philistinism of the art of "the golden mean"—the epigones of Tchaikovsky and the New Russian School'.

However, Prokofiev proceeded to adjust himself to his new environment. The same year he wrote successful music to the film *Lieutenant Kizhe* more or less in his old grotesque, satirical vein, and to the extraordinary theatrical entertainment that Alexander Tayrov, then director of the Moscow Chamber Theatre, concocted from Shaw's *Caesar and Cleopatra*, Pushkin's *Egyptian Nights* and Shakespeare's *Antony and Cleopatra*, and christened after the Pushkin story. And from both of these, in accordance with his favourite practice, he compiled 'symphonic suites' that have won considerable popularity. *Lieutenant Kizhe* has even been recorded for gramophone outside the U.S.S.R., though whether it is still officially approved inside the country I do not know; it was composed in 1934 and since then the campaign against artistic 'formalism' has been still further intensified. (In the sphere of the theatre, for instance, Tayrov—a brilliantly experimental producer —was dismissed from his post in 1937.) But Prokofiev's process of adjustment can, as I suggested earlier, be studied most clearly by looking at the first important work written after his acquisition of Soviet citizenship—the G minor Violin Concerto—and by comparing it with the first Violin Concerto in D major.

Now the D major Concerto is on the whole a lyrical work; the dreamy *andantino* first movement, with its *cantabile*, essentially diatonic principal theme, gives its *cachet* to the whole composition.

[1] The musically progressive Association for Contemporary Music which flourished in the 1920's.

In the last movement the soloist, after a brief threat of misbe-
haviour, settles down to a flexible, *cantabile* theme, and there is a
memorable, purely diatonic tune played by the violas; but there is
also a certain amount of the familiar Prokofievian naughtiness.
There is, for instance, a good deal of freakishness even in the first
movement; and the second movement is one of Prokofiev's most
brilliant scherzi, comparable with the dry, glittering, steely things
one remembers best in his piano concertos. That really is the
main difference between this work and the Second Concerto; there
is no naughtiness, there is no steely glitter, and there is almost no
virtuosity in the solo part. The first movement, though an *allegro*,
is entirely based on lyrical material and the middle movement,
instead of a scherzo, is an *andante assai*. So far as the violin-
concerto form is concerned, Prokofiev's formula for turning himself
into a Soviet composer has been to emphasize the lyrical side of his
nature at the expense of the witty and grotesque and brilliant sides.
(And not only in the Violin Concerto.) It is a simple prescription
and, though it has put a constraint on his creative nature, it has not
made him do violence to it. Indeed the repressed side of himself
has found some slight outlet. in this lyrical music through the

Ex. 14

exaggeration of an old innate tendency: to abrupt modulation—'tonal
dislocation', as Soviet critics call it.
(The *Vision fugitive*, Op.22, No. 8,
occurs to me as an early example and
the opening of *Petya and the Wolf*,
the 'Petya' theme itself [Ex. 14], as a

recent one.) The second subject of the *allegro moderato* of the G minor Concerto, worth quoting also for its distant affinity with the gavotte of the Classical Symphony, illustrates the 'exaggeration' of this tendency:

Ex. 15

All the same, the exorcising of the old *diablerie* leaves an impression of insipidity. The lyrical Prokofiev is delicious as a foil; it is not quite good enough to stand on its own; it is egg without salt.

This insipidity is specially notable in the *Romeo and Juliet* music—at any rate in the second of the two symphonic suites, which is all I know of it—though Soviet critics hailed it as the work in which Prokofiev had really turned toward the light. And I must confess to finding the now celebrated *Petya and the Wolf* a little insipid, too, though this has the excuse that it is pap for babes, not meat for adults, and even adults can wholeheartedly admire the ingenuity not only of the musical workmanship but of the manner in which Prokofiev has contrived to smuggle in quite a lot of thematic and harmonic contraband disguised as pictorialism for children: there are things in *Petya and the Wolf* that would have been condemned out of hand by orthodox Soviet critics as senseless modernism and 'formalism', if they had not been passed off as illustrations of Petya lassoing the wolf by its tail, or the wolf stalking the duck. As a 'symphonic tale for children' the piece, with its naïve pictorialism and naïve leitmotives and naïve instrumental characterization, is of course admirable.

So far, the most impressive of Prokofiev's Soviet compositions known to me is the cantata, *Alexander Nevsky*. (That statement may have to be modified when we get the scores of *Simeon Kotko* and the *War and Peace* opera; it would, I fancy, be unaffected by a hearing of the *Greeting to Stalin* based on the texts of Russian, Ukrainian, White Russian, Mordvinian, Kurdish and other national songs about Stalin, or of the *Cantata for the 20th Anniversary of the October Revolution* for orchestra, military band, accordeon band

and two choirs, with words compiled from the speeches and writings of Marx, Lenin and Stalin.) I have already spoken of Prokofiev's 'favourite practice' of piecing together symphonic suites from his operas and film-music and music for plays; *Alexander Nevsky* also originated in film-music—music for the great Eisenstein-Vasilev film of the overthrow of the Teutonic Knights at the Battle of Lake Peypus in 1242—but the cantata that resulted, a cycle of seven 'monumental symphonic frescoes' as it has been called, is much more than a suite of selected numbers. As long ago as 1914 Prokofiev had shown in the *Scythian Suite*, his gift for musical nationalism of the less superficial kind, for evoking Russia's barbaric and heroic past, and some of us have gone on wondering whether that *Suite* was not really his best work; his failure to follow it up has always been as disappointing as it was inexplicable. The *Russian Overture* of 1936 revived one's hopes and then, three years later, *Alexander Nevsky* to a great extent fulfilled them.

The first movement is a remarkable tone-picture of the vast, empty Russian landscape, remarkable above all for the economy of the means employed:

Ex. 16

The second, in which the chorus describes the previous exploits of Prince Alexander Nevsky in repelling a Swedish invasion,[1] is less striking; it is virile, straightforward and thoroughly Russian— one might easily mistake it for one of the choruses from *Sadko*, were it not for the unconventional methods[2] by which Prokofiev suggests the *gusli* and other national instruments; but its simplicity seems a little too deliberate:

EX. 17

('*And there was a fight on the Neva river, on the great water*')

Some years ago Prokofiev said, in reply to criticisms, that in *Romeo and Juliet* he had 'taken special pains to achieve a simplicity which will, I hope, reach the hearts of all listeners. If people find no melody and no emotion in this work of mine, I shall be very sorry; but I feel sure that they will sooner or later'; one feels that here again he has 'taken special pains to achieve simplicity'. The composer next paints the enemy, the Catholic Teutonic Knights gathered in Pskov, and it is worth while to quote his own words again:

[1] In a battle on the banks of the Neva, whence his epithet *Nevsky*: 'of the Neva.'
[2] Flutes, clarinets, saxophones and percussion, instead of Rimsky-Korsakov's harp-and-piano convention.

'As the action is laid in the thirteenth century I was above all interested to know what music was sung by the Catholics at that period. I got hold of a book containing a collection of Catholic chants of various periods, but this music was so strange to us that it was impossible to use it in the film. No doubt the Teutonic Knights, going into battle, sang it with frenzy but to modern ears it would have sounded cold and expressionless. So I was obliged to compose for the Knights music that would sound more apt to contemporary listeners.'

Accordingly the Catholic chant is given an iron cruelty quite foreign to the genuine music of the Roman Church. The massive, mail-clad Knights are painted with heavy brass and grinding dissonances; like the Big Bad Wolf in *Petya*, they provide an excellent pretext for modernity of idiom, and the climax of this scene is reached by the building-up of their archaic pentatonic fanfares into a polytonal complex. 'Apart from its context,' observes a Russian critic (Ostretsov—the same Ostretsov who had so unsparingly condemned the *Symphonic Song*), 'this episode would be meaningless; in the context it is exactly right.' Polytonality is permissible if you associate it with the enemy.

The fourth movement, 'Arise, O Russian people, for the glorious battle, the battle for life and death', is a counterpart to the second —and a better counterpart. Its simplicity seems more spontaneous; and if the music is not strikingly original, it is not unworthy of comparison with some of the best choral passages of *Prince Igor*:

Ex. 18

The fifth movement, the description of the battle on the
frozen lake, is the most film-like (and will vividly recall to those
who saw it the memorable scenes of Eisenstein's film); it begins
with the dawn scene—the mail-clad knights on their mail-clad
horses slowly crossing the ice as the sun rises—and depicts the
course of the battle with considerable realism and (again justified)
modernity:

Ex. 19

These harmonies and these dynamic 'motor' rhythms betray
the old 'Western' Prokofiev. But it must be said that the music
is not very good Prokofiev; film-music in the concert hall is the
worst kind of programme-music; only the end in this cantata-
version, the poetic reference to the previous movement, rises to the
higher level of the work.

The sixth movement, the beautiful lament of a Russian woman
on the battlefield at night, is completely on that higher level.
And the last movement, depicting Alexander Nevsky's triumphant
entry into Pskov, with bells ringing (as in so many classical Russian

scores), the cheers of the people and the pranks of jesters (again as in *Prince Igor* and other Russian classics), is a fine colourful picture. I give a quotation from it to show how Prokofiev contrives to add his personal touch to familiar Russian idioms:

Ex. 20

To sum up, then, I think it may be said that Prokofiev's development has not suffered very severely by his decision to return to his native land. It has been restricted in some directions, directions that many people believed—but believed wrongly—to represent the whole, or nearly the whole, of the essential Prokofiev. (Though, as we have seen, the composer has ingeniously contrived a few essays in these directions too, whenever he could find excuses for them.) And it has intensified his earlier tendency towards simplicity and lyrical melody. He has been deprived of much of his old pungency, but he has been encouraged to develop the epic vein he had neglected since the says of his *Scythian Suite*. Balancing gains and losses, I find it difficult to decide which are the more considerable. At any rate it may be said with confidence that he, the returned *émigré*, has not been cramped by the artistic policy of the Soviet Government to anything like the same extent as Shostakovich, who has grown up artistically with the Soviet state and might have been expected to adapt himself more easily to its requirements. But that is perhaps because Prokofiev is a much better composer than Shostakovich.

IV. ARAM KHACHATURYAN

WHEN MOURA LYMPANY gave the first English performance of Aram Khachaturyan's Piano Concerto at Queen's Hall on 13 April 1940, the very name of this young Armenian musician was, if not completely unknown, comparatively unfamiliar even to those in the audience who had always taken a special interest in Russian music. (I myself knew him only through a Trio for clarinet, violin, and piano, dating from 1932.) The Concerto proved to be no masterpiece but, all the same, an extremely attractive work; it had abundant life and plenty of colour, qualities that distinguished it from its neighbours in the programme, the Fifth Symphony of Shostakovich and the Sixteenth of Myaskovsky. Since then the Piano Concerto has been heard several times and confirmed that favourable initial impression; it has won what, for a contemporary work, must be accounted popularity. (It is very popular in Russia.)

Khachaturyan is a composer to be reckoned with, then. 'But who is he? What has he done?' one naturally wants to know, and questions like that about almost any Soviet composer are not easily answered. But for that invaluable monthly *Sovetskaya Muzïka* one would hardly be able to answer them at all, and I am indebted to a lengthy essay on Khachaturyan by Georgy Khubov, which appeared in *Sovetskaya Muzïka* (September 1939), for most of the following biographical details and for descriptions of works that have not yet reached this country.[1]

Aram Ilich Khachaturyan was born in Tiflis in 1904, his father being a bookbinder. Far from being an infant prodigy, he seems to have shown no particular aptitude for music—or at least took no serious interest in music—till he was nineteen. Then in the autumn of 1923 he appeared in Moscow at the well-known music school directed by the Gnesins and demanded musical education. He had no theoretical knowledge of music at all, no knowledge of the great

---

[1] Further biographical details are given in Y. Y. Baynkop's article on Khachaturyan in the booklet *Sovetskie Kompozitori* (Leningrad Philharmonia, 1938); there are discrepancies between some of his dates and Khubov's, but I have followed Khubov.

classical literature; he was even doubtful what particular branch of music to specialize in; he had only a profound inner conviction that he was a musician. However, he was admitted to the school and for two years studied the 'cello, until in 1925 M. F. Gnesin (himself a former composition pupil of Rimsky-Korsakov) accepted him in his composition class, where he worked so industriously that within a year he had produced a Dance for violin and piano mature enough to be published by the Music Section of the Armenian State Publishing Department. Mature enough to be printed, it should be noted, but not, of course, mature in any other sense. Yet, according to Khubov, this Dance in B flat, Op.1, and a Poem in C sharp minor, Op.3, for piano which appeared in 1927, both 'in oriental style', already show the qualities and defects of Khachaturyan's later manner: a fresh, spontaneous vein of melody largely inspired by the folk-music of the Caucasian and trans-Caucasian peoples, a tendency to loose, rhapsodic structure, a keen rhythmic sense and a love of warm, colourful sound effects.

The Khachaturyan of this period was in the position of an eager, intelligent child who has just been given the run of a toyshop. It is really very difficult to imagine oneself in the place of this young man in his early twenties, intensely musical, very gifted, yet who was belatedly making the acquaintance of the great composers all more or less at the same time. 'Everything was equally new to him: Bach and Ravel, Glinka and Skryabin.' And as was quite natural, it was the newest and gaudiest toys in the shop that caught his fancy first; like many other young musicians with fuller cultural backgrounds, Khachaturyan discovered music through contemporary music and only later developed a love of the classics. At that time, the late nineteen-twenties, the younger Russian musicians had not yet been isolated from their Western contemporaries by the Chinese Wall erected to shut out foreign formalism, intellectualism, and pessimism; there was free and healthy artistic intercourse between Russia and her not-yet-Nazified Western neighbours. The young Khachaturyan was particularly attracted by Ravel and the Central European 'expressionists' and their influence is said to be very strongly marked in some unpublished pieces written at this period; it is still evident, in fairly mild forms, in the Clarinet Trio and in still more mature works. But although orthodox Soviet critics shake their heads sorrowfully over these modest little crops produced by the wild-oat sowing of 1928-9, it must be said emphatically that the real Khachaturyan is far from being an 'advanced' composer as we understand 'advanced modernism' in Western Europe.

The reasons for this retreat from modernity are probably complex. No doubt the fundamental reason was Khachaturyan's discovery of his true creative self, which is essentially lyrical. He is intensely interested in folk-music, not only the music of his own Armenian race but that of the neighbouring peoples—not as a student of musical ethnography, but as a creative artist; even as a student he is said to have written some remarkable songs in the Turkoman, Armenian and Turkish idioms; and, despite the example of Bartók, love of folk-music is not easily reconciled with advanced modernism. But it is not improbable that this natural tendency was strengthened first by the later phase of Khachaturyan's musical education and then by official frowns on modernism in music.

In 1929 he left the Gnesins' school and entered the Moscow State Conservatoire where he stayed till 1934. Here he continued to study composition first under his old teacher M. F. Gnesin, then under Myaskovsky, and worked at orchestration with S. N. Vasilenko and N. Ivanov-Radkevich, at the same time busying himself with social musical work, particularly at the Moscow House of Culture of Soviet Armenia. The compositions of this period include a Sonata for violin and piano (1932), the already-mentioned Trio (also 1932), a five-movement *Dance-Suite* for full orchestra (1933), and a considerable number of 'compositions for the masses': songs, dances, pieces for balalayka, military marches and so on, of which the marches in particular are said to have won great popularity in the Red Army. Of these the most significant seems to be the Trio—loose and weak in structure, like so much of Khachaturyan's work, but abounding with rhythmic vitality, playing off the different types of cantilena natural to clarinet and violin (the clarinet predominates) against mainly percussive piano-writing:

Ex. 21

and possessing far more harmonic bite than either of the concertos. To Western ears the clashes of seconds, the side-slippings
of curiously built-up chords, and so on, will suggest affinities with
French impressionism and the milder Bartók but according to
I. Martïnov (article in *Sovetskaya Muzïka*, May 1938), 'the
composer himself says that in building up his complicated harmonic complexes he has attempted to reproduce the effects of
stringed folk-instruments. Undoubtedly many features of Khachaturyan's harmonic language can be explained by his striving
to develop to the full the modal peculiarities of the melodies
he has treated.' For, according to Martïnov, 'the Trio is

based on genuine folk-melodies'.[1] And, he adds, 'the multiform and interesting scales of these melodies often differ very considerably from the familiar major and minor'. On the other hand, Khubov speaks of Khachaturyan's 'constant endeavour to colour the folk-diatonic with chromaticisms. It is this which is partly responsible for the piquant tang of Khachaturyan's harmony.' It may seem difficult at first sight to reconcile these two expert judgments, but examination of one or two of Khachaturyan's scores shows that there is something to be said for both views: his harmony does make the most of the modal peculiarities of his material but it also supplies an element of spice on its own account.

This spice is decidedly less noticeable, though still present, in the First Symphony (1934) and the post-Conservatoire works: the Toccata for piano solo, the music for the film *Pepo*, the Piano Concerto (1936), the symphonic *Poem about Stalin* (1938), the ballet *Happiness* and the Violin Concerto (both 1940). Yet the thematic material of these works, though not, I believe, actually borrowed from the treasury of popular song—except in the case of *Happiness*, which introduces not only Armenian but Russian, Ukrainian and Georgian songs and dance tunes—is strongly influenced by the songs of the *ashugs*, the native bards of Armenia. (Khachaturyan's *Song Poem* for violin and piano, written in 1929, is inscribed 'In honour of the *ashugs*' and frankly imitates their improvisatory style of singing.) But on the whole, so far as one can judge from the few available scores and from Russian criticism, these later works tend to revert to a more conservative idiom and

[1] According to Khubov the theme of the finale:

Ex. 22

is an Uzbek melody.

it is not difficult to find in them affinities with Borodin and Tchaikovsky.

According to Khubov the most important of these works is the
three-movement Symphony: 'This fine composition, particularly
its first movement—a monumental *Allegro* with a broad introduction on improvisatory lines—may without any exaggeration be
described as an important peak not only in the composer's creative
career but in the general development of Soviet symphonism. The
role of this work in our symphonic music is no less important than
the role of Dzerzhinsky's opera, *Quiet Flows the Don*, in the art of
Soviet musical drama.' And that is saying a great deal, for *Quiet
Flows the Don* is, as I shall show in a later chapter, considered a
model Soviet opera. 'Khachaturyan's symphony is a lyrical-epic
structure; its content is a lofty epic of the new, strenuous, joyous
life of work and conflict.' That is to say, it is a model work ideo-
logically as well as, perhaps more than, musically. But Khubov is
too sound a critic to give a work such high praise solely on ideological grounds. And he gives the Symphony—at least the first
movement, which he considers 'a perfectly independent symphonic
poem'—very high praise indeed; the slow movement and finale,
he admits, do not sustain the impetus of the *Allegro*. His description
certainly arouses one's keen interest, for the Symphony seems to
present a number of striking structural features. For one: 'the
unity of diverse thematic material in development, in other words,
monothematism; Khachaturyan adheres to this principle in all his
important compositions.' Thus the prologue contains the basic
themes of the whole Symphony and the first theme of the *Allegro ma
non troppo* grows out of this prologue 'immediately and organically',
while the second main subject (which brings a change of tempo as
in Tchaikovsky's 'Pathétique', to *Andantino cantabile*) 'emerges
against a background provided by the dying away of a metamor-
phosis of the principal theme'. But despite this talk of first and
second subjects, the movement has little in common with traditional first-movement structure. The slightly Borodinesque first
subject is developed polyphonically at some length before the
second subject appears at all; this in turn, a decidedly Armenian
melody:

Ex. 23

Andantino cantabile

is developed harmonically and through play of orchestral colour.
The development is thus mixed up with the exposition; and
orthodox recapitulation is replaced by 'a powerful assertion
of the *unity* of the contrasted material', both themes, as well
as the rhapsodic melody of the prologue, being fused into a
single complex. (There is a partial precedent for this procedure in
Borodin's First Symphony.) The same material is worked out
further in the *Adagio sostenuto* and *Allegro risoluto*, notwithstanding
which (according to Khubov) they are suite-like in effect. The
physical unity of the whole Symphony is assured by the use of the
same material, but it lacks spiritual unity. Indeed Khubov condemns the finale for its monotony, its over-use of rich orchestral
colour and its repeated climaxes.

Khachaturyan's next big work after the Symphony was the now
fairly familiar Piano Concerto which admittedly never touches the
heights of the first movement of its predecessor. It shows Khachaturyan learning self-discipline but also losing a little of his indivi-
duality. Both the slow movement and the second subject of the first
movement (see Ex. 24 on p. 50) are somewhat Borodinesque, while
the dry, brilliant finale reminds one of Prokofiev. The first movement is quite orthodox in form. The more recent Violin Concerto
is on very similar lines, but sparer in texture and rather simpler in
build—though the solo part is anything but easy.

The two remaining major compositions of Khachaturyan of
which anything is known[1] are the *Poem about Stalin* and *Happiness*.
In 1937 Khachaturyan had been thinking of writing a symphonic
poem with final chorus, when he came across a poem, *A Song of*

---

[1] I have not yet heard or seen his Second Symphony.

Ex. 24

Stalin, written by the *ashug* Mirza Bayramov, one of the leading poets of the Soviet Republic of Azerbayjan, and made a choral setting of it; this was performed with great success at a festival of Soviet music in Moscow in November 1937, and quickly won wide popularity. Khachaturyan then wrote the score of a symphonic poem based on the same melody:

Ex. 25

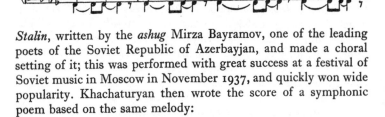

and introducing the choral song at its climax, and the complete *Poem about Stalin* was duly performed at the next annual festival in November 1938. These circumstances gave rise to the criticisms that the orchestral piece had been written to exploit the success of the song and that the choral finale did not arise naturally out of the symphonic fabric.

The *Poem about Stalin* presents a successful synthesis of characteristic traits of the national music of Armenia, Georgia, and Azerbayjan, and the music of the Third Act of the ballet *Happiness*[1] also symbolizes, though in a slightly different way, the brotherhood of the various races of the Soviet Union. Here actual folk-tunes are used, not merely 'characteristic traits'. The Armenian element predominates; the score contains no fewer than eight Armenian national melodies; but interwoven with them are themes representative of Russia proper (a song and dance tune), the Ukraine (a gopak) and Georgia (a lezginka). As in everything Khachaturyan has written so far, there are bad patches in *Happiness*: dull things, trivial things, things that suggest 'the melodramatic pathos of Rakhmaninov'. But on the whole the music is said to be genuinely 'symphonic', 'in the classical Russian tradition of the symphonic ballet scores of Borodin, Tchaikovsky and Glazunov'.

[1] The action of the ballet is described in Cyril W. Beaumont's *Supplement to Complete Book of Ballets* (Beaumont, 1942).

V. LEV KNIPPER

ALTHOUGH his music has little in common with Khachaturyan's, Lev Knipper's career has been strangely like the Armenian's. Born in the same city of Tiflis—but six years earlier (in December 1898) —Knipper, too, began to study music very belatedly (at the age of twenty-four); he too has shown considerable interest in the music of the sister-peoples of the U.S.S.R., particularly in that of the Tajiks; he too began as a modernist in the Western European sense, and turned to the ideals of 'music for the masses' and 'music of endeavour' only in 1932. But that Paul-like conversion was not peculiar to him and to Khachaturyan; it was a spiritual experience shared by a good many of their colleagues. According to Knipper himself,[1] 'the change was not a sudden one but the gradual result of persistent work on my *Weltanschauung*, work that was accompanied by a struggle to crystallize my style, a striving for the expression of a definite content'.

'Persistent work' has been the keynote of Knipper's life. 'My career has been one of intense labour and study', he has said himself. 'Sometimes as much as eighteen hours a day. I always realized that the demands of the age in which we live are so enormous that to start work on the new themes, without being well-armed technically and without attempting to find new means for the solution of the new problems, was unthinkable. The tendencies that I inherited from the old—a little of impressionism, a little of Tchaikovsky and more than was good for me—aesthetic refinements— was a heavy enough load, which I have not completely thrown off to this day. In a series of compositions in my short creative career (I began to study music only in 1924) I tried to break the chains of old forms, but—despite my warm desire and the help of my teacher, N. S. Zhilyaev—without success.' The compositions of this early period, in which (as Knipper himself puts it) he possessed 'insufficient skill to state my thoughts clearly, to handle my

[1] Article in *Muzikalnaya Samodeyatelnost* (October 1933). I am indebted to this, and to another article contributed to *Sovetskaya Muzika* in May of the same year, for a number of autobiographical particulars.

materials freely', include the orchestral *Tales of the Plaster Idol* (1925) and *Episodes of the Revolution* (1926), and the *Candide* suite for piano, Op. 16 (1927). In these he revealed that flair for the humorous, even the grotesque and satirical, which has always been one of his more striking traits.

Knipper's first really important work was the opera *North Wind* (1929), with a libretto by the well-known Soviet dramatist, Kirshon. But if 'really important' and quite characteristic of Knipper's slightly dry and cerebral tendencies, it is not at all typical of his mature work. The subject is a tragedy of the Civil War and 'intervention' period (I believe an historic incident), with heroic commissars, a wicked Menshevik and a villainous English commander. But Knipper's music is 'advanced' in the musical sense, and therefore regrettable from the Russian political point of view; it is music for the bourgeois intelligentsia. Far from being 'simple, sensuous, and passionate', it is harmonically sophisticated, dry, more than a little Hindemithian. It is entirely subordinated to the dramatic action, though not always in the most obvious of ways: 'according to Knipper's view,' explains one Russian critic, 'the music should "counterpoint" with the action, giving its inner content sometimes even contrary to its outward expression [on the stage].' There are only two really lyrical passages in the whole work, the songs of an *ashug* and of an oil-worker, the rest being clever but rather dry recitative (see Ex. 26 on p. 54).

Even in this tragic work, the satirical vein is not entirely suppressed.

In 1931 followed another opera, *Cities and Years* based on the famous novel by Konstantin Fedin, of which I have failed to discover any other particulars, and a curious set of *Four Children's Miniatures* for various small instrumental combinations: flute, viola, and tuba; flute, cor anglais, clarinet, trumpet, trombone, tuba, violin, viola and 'cello; clarinet, trumpet and 'cello; violin, cor anglais and trombone. In July of the same year Knipper was represented—by a *Lyric Suite* for small orchestra—at the Oxford I.S.C.M. Festival. But, before this, new influences had begun to make themselves felt in his music. Summers spent in the Central Caucasus in 1930 and in the Pamir Mountains of Tajikistan in 1931, 'not as a tourist, but working among the people, amid their

Ex. 26

('*It's I . . . How are you? . . . Well . . .*')

national songs . . . gave me infinitely much, above all gave me
understanding of the melodic source as fundamental.' The second
of these two visits was especially fruitful, for it gave rise to a whole
series of works based on Tajik themes: the orchestral suites,
Stalinabad (1931) and *Vanch* (1932), *Four Tajik Dances* for orchestra, a Tajik overture *Vakhio Bolo* and *Five Tajik Songs* for
piano (all 1933). The most successful of these is *Vanch*, perhaps the
most important of all the fairly numerous essays in the treatment
of Oriental folk-music by non-Oriental Russian composers.
Knipper's approach to his Tajik themes is quite different from that
of nineteenth-century Russian composers to Oriental material.
There is no picturesque Russification but a serious attempt to
evolve a more highly organized work of art from the essence of the
themes themselves; the necessary changes in the material sound
more like 'variants' (in the folk-song collector's sense) than 'variations'; the counterpoints are themselves evolved from the themes:

Ex. 27

A whole chapter might be written on Knipper's treatment of this interesting folk-material.[1]

'Work on form, on the simple and clear statement of my thoughts with the most economical means, work on small orchestral combinations, development of contrapuntal technique and a final renunciation of impressionistic models' had by this time brought Knipper to the verge of artistic maturity. And among the group of works written in 1932—including the lyrical Second Symphony, commemorating the fifteenth anniversary of the Revolution, the suite *Memories* for violin and orchestra, a Sinfonietta consisting of four pieces inspired by Charles de Coster's novel *Till Eulenspiegel* (which was followed next year by two *Eulenspiegel* song settings)— one composition stands out as the first really satisfactory embodiment on a large scale of Knipper's new artistic ideals: the Third (*Far Eastern*) Symphony. Knipper had already developed certain convictions about the symphony: that it should not stay confined by the limitations of traditional form but should adopt all possible means to express some fundamental idea (one is strongly reminded of Mahler), and that, if one is really to write 'symphonies for the masses', one must make at least some of the episodes singable by the masses, that 'in mass song there is nothing inherently opposed

[1] Indeed such an essay has been written—by V. Belyaev (*Sovetskaya Muzika*, April 1937).

to symphonism and that, treated as a symphonic theme, a mass
song may offer first-rate material for the working-out of an idea'.
The Second Symphony and the two Tajik suites were written with
these conceptions in mind but Knipper still sought 'a concrete
subject' for a great work, a subject about which he could crystallize
the results of the previous years of experiment. This subject was
at last suggested by a visit to the Red Army of the Far East in the
summer of 1932, when Knipper acted as musical instructor to
the troops, conducted army choirs and shared the daily life of
the men.

The result, the *Far Eastern* Symphony, is a five-movement work
for full orchestra, military band, soloists and male choir, in the
direct line of descent from the symphonies of Berlioz (*Roméo et
Juliette* and the *Symphonie funèbre et triomphale*) and Mahler. The
'concrete subject' was, after all, not so very concrete; it was, rather,
a general impression of the life and work of the Army of the Far
East and its campaign on the Manchurian frontier in 1929, plus a
certain amount of musical landscape painting and ethnology.
(Knipper had been noting down Buryat folk-music.) The slow first
movement washes in the background, the dreary waste of steppe,
and its principal theme, the long-drawn, flexible melody of the
muted violas, with which the Symphony opens:

Ex. 28

recurs in the later movements as a sort of 'steppe' motive. Then a
Buryat melody is heard, sung off-stage, and a third more or less
elegiac theme is announced by the horns. The music came to
Knipper as he stood on the bank of the River Argun, which marks
the frontier of the U.S.S.R. The *allegro* second movement is frankly
a battle-picture; the 'steppe' theme is transmogrified in familiar
nineteenth-century style:

Ex. 29
Allegro
(Vln.)

ff

a muted trumpet introduces a fanfare-like symbol of the Red Army,
and the coda finally ties these two themes and the Buryat song into a
skilful contrapuntal knot. The third movement is a rather weak
funeral march, a salute to fallen comrades; the fourth, a lively *allegro
scherzando* depicting the lighter side of Red Army life (comradeship
and healthy laughter) and introducing a *chastushka* (topical popular
song), 'The Dashing General'. The 'steppe' theme also returns in
its original form. The finale is based on a mass marching song in
which Knipper, 'in an ideal performance of the Symphony', would
like the audience to join; the idea was to crown the Symphony with
a great, broad, popular song of pride and joy, to some extent on the
lines of Beethoven's Choral Symphony; the 'steppe' and 'Red Army'
themes are interwoven and the whole culminates in a tremendous
climax of sound. The *Far Eastern* Symphony is no masterpiece. It
does not really hold together; only the first two movements are
genuinely symphonic; the funeral march is weak (Knipper has rewritten both this and the second movement, more than once); the
marching song of the finale is almost incredibly banal:

Ex. 30
Marziale

Za   dal'- ne - vos-toch - noy   gra - ni - tse - yu   sle -

- dit   ne - us -tan - no   o - na

('*Unwearying it watches on the Far Eastern frontier*')

Yet the thing has power and is, above all, interesting as a fairly
early example of the type of lyrical, ideological music characteristic
of more recent Soviet tendencies.

Since the *Far Eastern* Knipper has produced at least four other symphonies. The Fourth (1933), sub-titled 'Four études for orchestra: improvization, march, aria, finale', shows a certain backsliding from orthodox Soviet musical ideology but has many points of interest. Traditional principles of form and thematic development are treated with scant respect, but the actual stuff of the music betrays its Tchaikovskian ancestry. But the real clue to the work lies in the sub-title; like the earlier *Children's Miniatures*, it is a series of studies in orchestral sound, studies for a curiously constituted orchestra of single wood-wind, one horn, one trumpet, and no second violins. Thus the 'improvization' is essentially a study for strings; the outstanding point of the 'aria' is a duet for trumpet and trombone; and so on. The Fifth Symphony (1933–4),[1] however, reverts to the style and partly to the methods of the Third; entitled *Poem about the Komsomols* (i.e. the Union of Communist Youth), it is a lyrical-epic work with a programme glorifying Communist ideology.

The composer himself has given us a long and detailed account[2] of the ideas underlying the Symphony and their musical embodiment: 'In 1918 I knew a young man who joined a guerrilla band to fight for the Soviets. He had a mother who loved him dearly and did not understand why he had to leave her. He too loved her and the parting cost him great pain. However, he joined the guerrillas, armed with youth and strength and the romance of the struggle for a bright future. In one of the fights with the White Guards he was killed. The woman was left alone, sadly remembering her son, her only hope and pride. That is the subject of the first three movements. The finale is based on something I saw myself one spring: at a flourishing collective farm arrived an army of *komsomols* armed with their youth and strength and all the mighty technique of our Red Army. I remembered the young man, I remembered the guerrillas, I remembered all the hard years of fighting. And it seemed to me that this meeting of our youth, the young collective farmers and the young soldiers, full of strength and knowledge and

[1] Some confusion has arisen about the numbering of Knipper's symphonies. This is sometimes spoken of as the Fourth, the *Four Etudes* not being counted, while another 'Fifth' (*Lyrical Poem*) seems to have been suppressed.

[2] Quoted by I. Rizhkin in an article on 'Soviet symphonism' in *Sovetskaya Muzika*, June 1935.

confidence in a radiant future—that this was the best memorial to the young man, the best acknowledgment to those women who gave what they loved most for the Revolution.'

But how is all this treated in terms of music? Judging from the composer's own description (I have not seen the score), rather naïvely. 'The symphony has a fundamental brass motive, which begins it and underlies the whole composition: this is the theme of life. The broad introduction in the brass outlines it first. From it is born the characteristic theme of youth; after a short development, fragments of a guerrilla song are heard sung by a soloist. The theme of youth comes into conflict with the song . . .' and so on. Presently the lyrical theme of love intervenes and the musical drama is worked out in accordance with the programme; the guerrilla song finally fades away in the distance, and the first movement ends with dying echoes of the theme of maternal love (solo violin). The second movement suggests the coming fight and soon the song of the White Guards is heard; their frivolity is suggested by a trivial *chansonette* tune, their ferocity by the scoring (strings *col legno*, muted brass, use of lower registers, etc.) (Knipper obviously seized with pleasure this pretext for the grotesque and satirical.) A quiet lyrical episode reminds the hearer of what the Soviet troops are fighting for, and then the White Guard music returns and the guerrillas' song is heard in the distance. The movement passes without a break into the third: a funeral march, or rather a funeral ode to the fallen hero and an expression of the woman's grief. Again the guerrillas' song is heard at the end. The finale, in which a chorus is introduced, paints the scene on the *kolkhoz* (collective farm). A short introduction, based on the motive of life, leads to a gay movement woven from a *kolkhoz* song, a comic *chastushka* about an unlucky brigadier, the *komsomols*' march and, at the very end, the guerrillas' song, in various permutations and combinations.

Soviet critics have often complained of the wide differences between Knipper's own material and the popular songs he has introduced in the Third and Fifth Symphonies. There was, perhaps, an underlying suspicion that he was always a modernist at heart and that these naïve programme symphonies, with their quotations of banal patriotic songs, were not the real Knipper. The Sixth

Symphony (1936), which is 'pure' music, despite its dedication to the Red Cavalry, was greeted with a storm of abuse. 'Dry, abstract melodic language,' 'Formalistic nonsense,' 'scandalous sound-pyrotechnics,' 'degradation of the role of a symphony orchestra to the playing of noisy, eccentric circus-tricks,' 'anti-artisticness,' 'absence of ideas': these are only a few of the epithets hurled at the unlucky No. 6. In the Seventh (1939), Knipper seems to have compromised to some extent by again taking an ideological theme, a theme that became very fashionable at about that time: 'the defence of the Soviet land.' But he failed all the same to satisfy the critics that he had risen to the theme quite as a good Soviet composer should. There are three movements, each based on a motto-theme said to bear an unhappy resemblance to the motto-theme of Tchaikovsky's Fourth Symphony, but the programme is simpler and less precise than that of No. 5, of which one writer has observed that 'the music follows the programme as a film follows its scenario'. In No. 7 we are given only (1) the threat of war interrupting the peaceful life of the community, and the community's prompt reaction, (2) the victims of war, an elegy on fallen heroes (strangely interrupted by a dance-like episode), (3) conflict; triumph of the Red Army.

In dwelling at length on Knipper's symphonies, I have left myself no space to deal with his songs, which include a cycle of Pushkin settings, *Of Love*, for voice, string orchestra, flute, oboe, clarinet and bassoon. Nor have I been able to discover any particulars of the opera based on an episode from Pavlenko's novel, *In the East*, and dealing with guerrilla fighting on the Manchurian border, on which Knipper was working in 1938. Originally entitled *Mariya*, after the heroine (who does not appear in Pavlenko at all), it has since been re-named *The Rising Sun*; but I know nothing of its musical tendencies, nor even whether it has been staged. But it is primarily as a symphonist that one thinks of Knipper, and if I were asked to label him for handy reference I should not hesitate very long to stamp him 'the Mahler of Soviet Russia'. As we shall see in a moment, other Soviet composers have essayed the Mahlerian type of symphony; but with the doubtful exception of Shostakovich, none possesses anything like that rather literary vein of melancholy irony which makes Knipper seem so spiritually akin to Mahler.

VI. VISSARION SHEBALIN

VISSARION SHEBALIN is one of the most representative of Soviet composers. Like his teacher, Myaskovsky (who, even more than Glière, is the 'model' composer of the older generation of Soviet musicians), he seems to have a natural gift for that somewhat Tchaikovskian vein of melody which is now looked upon so favourably in the U.S.S.R. He has nothing of Knipper's and Shostakovich's tendency to intellectualism and experiment; he is not a folk-music-exploiter like Khachaturyan. He is simply a Russian—he was born at Omsk in 1902 and spent the whole of his youth there, studying music (and agriculture) till 1923—who writes the sort of music one expects a Russian to write: lyrical, technically fluent, individual but not startlingly so. Shebalin's creative career began directly with his move to Moscow and the commencement of his studies under Myaskovsky at the Conservatoire there. The first of his three string quartets, his Op.2, was written the same year (1923); the String Trio, Op.4, followed the year after; and in 1926 came the first Symphony in F minor. Shebalin's most important work has followed the directions indicated by those pointers. In 1933 he was said to be working on an opera, *The Lay of Opanas*, based on a poem by Bagritsky dealing with the Civil War in the Ukraine,[1] in which the principal musical element was to be 'song based on the intonations of folk-music'; and in 1938 reports told of his composition of another Civil War opera, *Comrades in Battle*, on a libretto by Vsevolozhsky and Y. Galitsky founded on the exploits of the 1st Cavalry Army. Some excerpts from the latter were performed at a Conference on Soviet Opera held in Moscow in May 1939, and

[1] According to Gleb Struve (*Soviet Russian Literature*), who considers Bagritsky 'one of the most talented and original of the young Soviet poets', the *Lay* is 'the story of a Ukrainian peasant who flies from the Communist food-detachment commanded by the Jew Kogan, encounters on his way the "Green" anarchist bands of Makhno and is forced to join them. Then Kogan is taken prisoner by the Makhno bands and Opanas is despatched to shoot him. On the way to the execution he changes his mind and proposes to Kogan to let him escape, but Kogan chooses death. Later on the Makhno bands are defeated by the Reds and Opanas in his turn taken prisoner. Questioned by the Red commander Kotovsky he confesses to having killed Kogan and submits docilely to the execution. It is a typical revolutionary heroic poem.'

warmly praised for the 'correctness of the path chosen by the
composer ... the simplicity of the musical idiom, the expressiveness
of the vocal parts, the emotionalism,' and the sharp characterization,
but I have not been able to trace any record of the production of
either this or the earlier opera. Shebalin has also essayed various
other forms: a Horn Concertino (about 1928), a Violin Concerto
(1936), a couple of orchestral Suites (the second begun in 1938),
two song-cycles, *Five Sonnets from Sappho*, Op.3, and a cycle of
Pushkin settings (1935), as well as a number of separate songs, a
Sonata, a Rondo, Op.8, and Three Sonatinas, Op.12, for piano
(early works), and music for plays and films (including one based
on Gogol's *Revizor*). But he has put the best of himself into his
quartets and symphonies, and it will be most convenient to discuss
these two groups separately, particularly as the First Quartet shows
Shebalin at his starting-point.

This Op.2 is in three movements; it reveals various influences,
that of Myaskovsky (which one would expect) and that of Prokofiev,
e.g. in the bustling opening theme of the finale:

Ex. 31

(which one would not); and it is hardly a model of quartet-style,
for the texture is too little polyphonic and rather too much first-
violin-solo - with - harmonic-background-broken-up-in-characteris-
tic-figuration:

Ex. 32

Moreover this harmony is a shade more spicey than that of Shebalin's more mature works. 'None the less,' comments K. Kuznetsov,[1] 'we already see in this quartet signs of the composer's own musical thinking, traits that are still perceptible in his most recent work. Above all, in the actual thematic material of the First Quartet there are features that show a relationship to the Third—particularly to those moments in the latter marked by broad tranquil Russian melody. From his very first quartet-opus Shebalin showed himself a forward-looking composer. He had already thrown off the domination of old artistic conceptions. The romantic style of the nineteenth century, the rhapsodic, the improvizatory, capricious unexpectedness—all this had little attraction for Shebalin. Characteristic of the style of the First Quartet is the tendency to great thematic concentration, to profundity of working-out, to shapely, well thought-out construction. One can speak of classical traits in Shebalin, but with this reservation: that contrapuntal methods play a more important role in his music than was permitted by the old classicism that was trying to free itself from the bonds of counterpoint. Imitations and canonic methods never threaten to overburden Shebalin; he uses them easily and readily.'

Shebalin's Second Quartet, Op.19, is a much riper work, dating from 1934. The first English performance was given by the Hirsch Quartet at the Æolian Hall on 13 December 1941, when it was rather overshadowed by Shostakovich's Op.49. But Russian critics consider it 'an important experiment in the history of Soviet chamber music'. Kuznetsov says of the *Andante cantabile* third movement: 'I do not hesitate to call this movement one of the most remarkable pages not only of Shebalin's work but of Soviet chamber literature in general. One hardly knows which to admire most: the breadth and warmth of the lyricism, the long-breathed melodies, the ideal balance of the parts or the superb treatment of the instruments.' And this in spite of modernist tendencies in the harmony, which however 'is not atonal (although there is not a single key-signature in the whole quartet), though not academic major-minor. It is a manifestation of a new tonal thinking, the quest for which may be observed—in certain hints—even in the pages of Shebalin's First Quartet.' The second movement is a rather trivial

[1] In an article on the quartets in *Sovetskaya Muzika*, January 1940.

scherzo (Kuznetsov condemns its 'mechanical and monotonous movement'), the fourth a vigorous *Allegro risoluto* harking back at the end to the first subject of the first movement.

The Third Quartet (1939), which bears no opus-number, is described by the composer himself as 'in E minor' though there is no sharp in the key-signature:

Ex. 33

and the F sharps that do occur are only chromatic alterations; the F naturals are far more numerous. However, to quote Kuznetsov once more, 'it would be wrong to speak here of the Phrygian mode in the true sense, since in the course of development the theme loses its initial diatonicism; on the other hand, it would also be wrong to ignore the influence on Shebalin's music of the old modes, transmitted through the medium of Russian folksong and the classics of Russian music (on whom, particularly on Glinka and Mussorgsky, Shebalin has spent a great deal of work). The influence of the West, during the period of work on the Second Quartet, did not make Shebalin an atonalist, but it undoubtedly acted as a ferment, an impulse to the search for new scale-formations. In the Third Quartet may be seen the process of crystallization of the new mode, in the formation of which many diverse elements play a part: both the old modes and new combinations, including the 12-tone scale. The old modes are treated as a firm canvas on which are painted the most diverse chromatic patterns'. That is how it appears to an intelligent Russian critic; to Westerners, accustomed to more highly spiced fare, the old in the quartet will be more apparent than the new, though it should be added that Shebalin has the power of conceiving new and beautiful themes in the old idiom (particularly in the *andante* and finale [see Ex. 34 on p. 65] of this quartet). The first movement is pleasantly laconic, but could hardly be anything else, considering the simplicity of the material, the scherzo attractive (one of Shebalin's best scherzi), the finale—as in the Second Quartet—

Ex. 34

the true culmination of the work, at least in intention, with numerous thematic references to the earlier movements.

Of Shebalin's First and Second Symphonies I know nothing, except that they were completed in 1926 and 1928 respectively (falling, therefore, between the First and Second Quartets); that the First is monothematic in structure (or at least based on metamorphoses of a few thematic elements) and romantically subjective in feeling; and that the Second, said to be a much better and more individual work, as one would expect, was played at the Prague I.S.C.M. Festival in 1935. (In passing, I would however, like to draw attention to the Concertino for horn and small orchestra, written at about the same time as the Second Symphony: a pleasant work in pastoral vein in which Shebalin is already, as in the Symphony, to be found experimenting with unusual scales.) The Third and Fourth Symphonies are more notable compositions. Indeed the Third, the *Lenin* (1934), is, I believe, considered one of the most important of contemporary Russian symphonies. The composer himself has described its origin:[1] 'The first thought of a great musical composition on the text of Mayakovsky's poem "Vladimir Ilich Lenin"[2] was expressed by the late author of the poem at one of the rehearsals of "Bani" at the Meyerhold Theatre, for which I was then writing music.[3] The suggestion was that I should take for my text the last section of the poem—Lenin's death. Nothing came of it at the time, owing to my inability to find any starting-point. It seemed to me that the task would reduce me to the role of

[1] Article in *Sovetskaya Muzika*, January 1933; a detailed analysis of the symphony, by A. Ostretsov, appeared in the same journal in March 1934.
[2] Which provided the basis of the symphony which Shostakovich was reported to have begun in 1940.
[3] Two songs from the music written for Meyerhold's production of Pushkin's *Stone Guest* are included in the Pushkin cycle mentioned above.

E

illustrator of the text and would allow me no scope to lay out a composition on monumental lines. Later on I more than once returned to this idea of a big symphonic composition to Mayakovsky's text, but the plan I finally adopted matured only in the spring of 1932. The first movement of the work, covering in very compressed form the first section of the poem, was written in the summer of the same year. The general layout of the symphony is as follows:

'I Introductory.
'II The year 1905 and the World War.
'III The October Revolution.
'IV Lenin's death and conclusion of the symphony.

'The proposed length of the symphony is about two hours; thus the complete work will demand a whole evening for its performance.'

Thus we are once more confronted with a vast Berliozian or Mahlerian conception, for narrator, soloists, chorus and orchestra, like Knipper's *Far Eastern* and *Komsomol* symphonies. As I have already pointed out, this genre has been enjoying considerable popularity in Soviet Russia in recent years. Revival of the symphonies of Mahler and Berlioz (including the *Symphonie funèbre et triomphale*) has come side by side with the creation of new works of this type, and it is not at all fanciful to trace a parallel with the 'monumental' musical tendencies of Revolutionary and Napoleonic France, of which Berlioz himself was the belated culmination. So far only two of these Russian 'dramatic symphonies' have been heard in this country—Shaporin's and the *Leningrad* of Shostakovich—and neither was an unqualified success. Nor have we ever taken kindly, much less rapturously, to the symphonies of Berlioz and Mahler. But if we are to make anything at all of the music of our Soviet allies, we must make at least an effort to appreciate this, perhaps the most characteristic of its forms.

Shebalin's approach is very different from Knipper's. He is less intellectual in tendency; he has nothing of that irony which underlines Knipper's spiritual affinity with Mahler; he is by nature a more lyrical composer. It should have been easier for him to write naturally in the right vein. But, judging from Ostretsov's article, which is copiously illustrated with music-type (I have not seen a score), Shebalin's lyricism is of the wrong type, too elegiac, insufficiently 'heroic' for the theme:

Ex. 35

As Ostretsov puts it: 'Shebalin is an outstanding master and should know that the means of expression suitable for the tone-painting of water-colour landscapes and melancholy nocturnes cannot be mechanically used for the heroic epoch of the Revolution. Hence we are genuinely puzzled when we hear the crystal, transparent sonority of his orchestra, from which it seems he has deliberately excluded everything that can convey a sense of power, everything manly and fullblooded, and left only transparent ghosts which evaporate and disappear, trailing over this instrumental landscape whirling puffs of harmonic smoke.' It also seems from Ostretsov's detailed analysis that Shebalin to some extent modified his original plan. The Symphony now consists of only three main parts, though the first of these alone—the introductory section intended to 'guide the listener into the circumstances of the revolutionary movement, to give the historical perspective of the Revolution and to give some idea of the threads that connected Lenin with the working class'— consists of three lengthy movements: an overture in sonata-form, suggesting 'the crisis of imperialistic society and the growth of the workers' movement', an elegy expressing the affection of the workers for their dead leader, a third movement 'devoted to the developing revolutionary situation'. They are bound together by community of material, which is often modified in familiar nineteenth-century style; thus the opening of the first movement:

Ex. 36

is thundered out in the second by a brass band of six trumpets and six trombones, *plus* orchestral brass:

Ex. 37

and is sung by the chorus in the finale:

Ex. 38

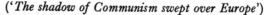

Kom - mu - niz - ma   priz - rak po Ev - ro - pe   ris - kal

(*'The shadow of Communism swept over Europe'*)

Shebalin's Fourth Symphony (1936) is dedicated 'to the heroes of Perekop'. (The storming of the Perekop Isthmus in 1920 was one of the most heroic events of the Civil War.) Like its predecessor, it has been criticized on the ground of thematic inadequacy. 'The language of this composition of Shebalin's,' says one critic, 'does not rise to the level of that deep simplicity'—I translate literally— 'and clear expressiveness which are indispensable in such a work as a symphony dedicated "to the heroes of Perekop".' The best that this writer, N. Chemberji, can find to say of it is that it is better than Knipper's Sixth Symphony—which is damning with the faintest possible praise. The *Perekop* Symphony is in two movements only: the first slow, in the favourite *héroïque-funèbre* vein, the second, an *allegro* in sonata-form, is more or less frankly programme-music describing the battle. Shebalin introduces in the Symphony the theme of his own song, 'On the Third Crimean Division'.

No account of Shebalin would be complete without some mention of his work on the unfinished compositions of nineteenth-century Russian musicians. I have already quoted Kuznetsov's remark that he 'has spent a great deal of work on the classics of Russian music, particularly on Glinka and Mussorgsky'. Shebalin has completed compositions by both these masters; the latter's *Sorochintsy Fair* (1933) and the former's *Symphony-Overture*[1] (1938). The version of *Sorochintsy Fair* that we have recently heard in London, the version that Albert Coates gave us at Covent Garden in 1936, is N. N. Cherepnin's, who solved the problem of completing Mussorgsky's torso by disregarding his scenario, sometimes using the existing music in the wrong place, and filling up the remaining gaps by adapting other music by Mussorgsky; Shebalin, like Cui before him, adopted the other course of preserving the action and existing music as Mussorgsky had intended, and composing the necessary additions himself. One would like to hear it— and also the Glinka piece, which is said to be based on two Russian melodies, one slow, the other a dance tune, like the well-known *Kamarinskaya* written fourteen years later.

---

[1] A composition begun by Glinka in Berlin in 1834, when he was studying with Siegfried Dehn.

VII. DMITRY KABALEVSKY

Hitherto I have discussed composers who, although they have written music for the stage and screen, have—with the possible exception of Shostakovich in his *Lady Macbeth of Mtsensk*—done their best work in the fields of symphony, concerto and chamber music. Kabalevsky has cultivated these fields, too; he has produced four symphonies; his Second Piano Concerto is the only serious rival to Khachaturyan's in the race to surpass Prokofiev; one of his piano sonatinas has been played a number of times in this country. Nevertheless, his real importance in contemporary Russian music is based on his opera, *The Master of Clamecy*, inspired by Romain Rolland's novel, or cycle of stories, *Colas Breugnon*.

Kabalevsky was born at St. Petersburg in 1904 and studied at the Moscow Conservatoire. He worked at the piano under A. B. Goldenweiser, friend of Leo Tolstoy, Skryabin and many other prominent figures of pre-Revolutionary Russia, and composition under Myaskovsky. Like the latter, he is much more prolific than the majority of modern composers; he began to compose at twenty-one and by the time he was twenty-six the list of his compositions included a String Quartet, Op.8, a Piano Concerto, Op.9, Two Songs on poems by Blok, Op.4, Eight Children's Songs, Op.17, and a whole group of works for piano solo: Four Preludes, Op.5, a Sonata, Op.6, Two Sonatinas, Op.13, and a set of five easy pieces *From Pioneer Life*, Op.14 ('Pioneers' are the Soviet equivalent of Boy Scouts and Girl Guides). Of these I know only the first of the two Sonatinas, a perky and attractive little three-movement work with a lyrical *andantino* that pays homage to Myaskovsky (and also touches its hat to the Ravel of *Ma Mère l'Oye*): (see Ex. 39 on p. 71.)

The music is diatonic, with no more harmonic pungency than can be extracted from progressions of chords of the seventh, added-note chords and the like. But the thing has savour. The Sonatinas are typical of one quite important side of Kabalevsky's work: his music for children. During 1925–6 he was engaged in teaching the piano to young children in a government school and was struck by the almost complete lack in Russia at that period of suitable material: very

Ex. 39
Andantino

easy pieces that would help children to conquer technical difficulties and at the same time begin to form their taste. He set out to fill the gap himself, the best of his pieces being published later in the set *From Pioneer Life*. Later, similar practical considerations led to the composition of his *Children's Songs*, Op.17. Kabalevsky does not regard the composition of educational music as mere hack-labour, for he has written more than one thoughtful and interesting essay on its special problems.

The Sonatinas were written in 1930; in the following year Kabalevsky produced the first of his more lasting major works, a *Poem of Struggle* for chorus and orchestra, which may be regarded as an essay in that type of choral symphony cultivated by Knipper, Shaporin, Shebalin and others; and in 1932 came Kabalevsky's First Symphony actually so called, composed like Myaskovsky's Twelfth in commemoration of the fifteenth anniversary of the October Revolution and, like it too, inspired by Viktor Gusev's poem, 'Proletarians of all lands, unite!' In a similar vein is the *Requiem* for Lenin, for chorus and orchestra, written in 1933 with words by N. Aseev and afterwards rather misleadingly styled 'Third Symphony'; its second movement is a march in that *funèbre et triomphale* style to which I have already drawn attention in the symphonies of Shebalin and Knipper. According to Ostretsov, both the First and Third Symphonies are marked 'by the purely eclectic use of thematic material of diverse character and by camouflage of outwardly correct thematic working-out, but also by routine methods in the actual structure of the symphony'. And he goes on to show that these weaknesses, shared by other Russian symphonies of the same period—e.g. Shekhter's (1931) and the Second and

Third Symphonies of Shostakovich (1927 and 1929)—are due to the composers having rejected classical symphonic principles, without replacing them by 'new, well thought-out architectural principles'. 'These defects were afterwards felt by the composers themselves. In their next symphonies' (i.e. Shostakovich's Fifth and Kabalevsky's Second) 'they are seeking the way to monumental forms employing the principles of the classical symphony. . . . In his Second Symphony Kabalevsky has achieved considerable expressiveness in the middle movement, full of feeling and rising in places to dramatic pathos; there is fire, too, in the impetuous finale with its witty variations, its dance rhythms and its effective scoring. The first movement is weaker; that it fails to carry conviction is due to the purely superficial contrast between first and second subjects, and to the thematic working-out which shows traces of a certain indifference, of academic insensibility.' This 'Second' (really, third) Symphony in C minor, written about 1934, was introduced to Western Europe in 1936 by Albert Coates, who conducted a performance in Vienna and a B.B.C. broadcast; the impression made on the majority of Western critics was of a talented work in the Tchaikovsky tradition, music in the polished lyrical style to which Arensky and Myaskovsky have accustomed us. The most striking movement was found to be the dancing scherzo which runs without a break into the more marchlike finale. (When Ostretsov speaks of 'the middle movement', of course, he means the *andante*, an interesting combination of rondo and variation forms.)

Soon after the Second Symphony came the Second Piano Concerto in G minor, which is generally considered one of Kabalevsky's best works. 'An enormous distance separates this talented composition from the unripe, studentlike, completely eclectic First Concerto,' observes one Russian critic. The Concerto is a three-movement work on more or less classical lines, but with several points of special interest. For instance, the idea which figures as the principal theme of the first movement:

Ex. 40

and (changed on what we are wrongly accustomed to think of as Lisztian lines) of the toccata-like finale, embodies one of the most striking peculiarities of Kabalevsky's style: the use of the major subdominant chord in a minor key. (In this case, effective play is made with the juxtaposition of major and minor subdominants.) At the end of the first movement occurs a simple and effective synthesis of first- and second-subject material, which perhaps owes its parentage to the parallel passage in Borodin's First Symphony. The solo-writing is beautifully pianistic and transparent; indeed, transparency, not to say simplicity, of texture is characteristic of Kabalevsky's music in general. His talent is essentially lyrical and he sets his lyrical outpourings against backgrounds that never threaten to overwhelm them.

The only major instrumental work that he has produced since the Second Concerto, so far as I have been able to discover, is the Fourth Symphony (1939). This bears the title *Shchors*, the name of a famous Red Army leader in the Civil War, and is a choral symphony, but I have not been able to discover anything about its programme or whether the music has any connection with that to Dovzhenko's *Shchors* film which Kabalevsky had composed just before; probably it has. (Incidentally he also wrote the music for *Petersburg Night*, and for Dovzhenko's *Aerograd* in 1935.)

Kabalevsky's stage works include two ballets, *Vasilek* (1938), and *Bïvaytse zdarovï* (1940). Both are said to deal with life on a collective farm and, scores not being available, I should suspect them of being one and the same work but that the libretto (*sic*) of the former is said to be by Grigoriev, that of the latter by E. M. Pomeshchikov. But these are evidently of slight importance by comparison with *The Master of Clamecy* (completed in 1937 and produced ʼhe following year) which is considered Kabalevsky's masterpiece.

Rolland's *Colas Breugnon* (or *Brugnon*, for the author himself spells it in both ways) is a singularly unpromising opera subject. The book consists of the month-by-month reflections through one year of a well-to-do Burgundian worker, a master craftsman in the early sixteenth century. There are incidents rather than a plot, though some of the incidents are exciting enough; they include a siege, a riot, and a fire. And naturally there are other characters

seen through Breugnon's keen eyes: his shrewish wife, his daughter
Martine and her husband, his favourite granddaughter Glodie, his
friends Paillard the notary and Chamaille the curé of Brèves, and
a considerable number of minor figures. But the one fully drawn
character, and the real subject of the book, is Colas himself: his
rich, laughing philosophy of life, his wise, salty humour, his wit,
his fire, his pride in his craft, his cunning, his sturdy bearing of
misfortune. In other words the real subject of the book is incapable
of being represented or expressed on the operatic stage. But the
evasion of that difficulty was only one of the problems lightly
solved by the ingenious librettist (V. Bragin). Rolland himself
described his book as 'sans politique, sans métaphysique, une livre
à la "bonne françoise", qui rit de la vie, parce qu'il la trouve bonne,
et qu'il se porte bien.' And that is true enough. But in the second
chapter Colas lets fall an observation much too savoury to escape
the keen nose of a good Communist:

'Mais qui ne dira pourquoi ont été mis sur terre tous ces
animaux-là, ces genpillehommes, ces politiques, ces grands seig-
neurs, qui de notre France sont saigneurs, et, sa gloire toujours
chantant, vident ses poches proprement, qui non rassasiés de
ronger nos deniers, prétendent dévorer les greniers étrangers,
menacent l'Allemagne, convoitent l'Italie, et dans le gynécée du
grand Turc fourrent leur nez, qui ne sauraient pas même y planter
des choux! . . . Allons, paix, mon ami, ne te fais point de bile!
Tout est bien comme il est . . . en attendant qu'un jour nous le
fassions meilleur (ce sera le plus tôt qu'il nous sera possible).'

This aside, for it is little more, becomes one of the basic ideas
of the operatic version, The Duke, who is only a 'noise off' in
Rolland, becomes the symbolical villain of the opera. When asked
to give his permission, however, Rolland had stipulated only 'don't
make Colas too serious. Colas without laughter won't be Colas.
For the rest—*carte blanche*. Fly with your own wings.' Accordingly
Bragin flew some distance.

In the book Colas is a man in the fifties; in the opera he is a
young man, a circumstance which makes a clean sweep of Martine
and Glodie and the shrewish wife. One chapter of the book shows
him visiting quite by chance one of his early loves, Belette, on a
lovely May morning; she had married the wrong man; the meeting

is described very beautifully, poignantly and without sentimentality; its function in the book is to show only one more side of Colas's character. In the opera, Belette becomes the youthful heroine, her name being Russianized into Lasochka (though she is also called Germaine). Act I consists of two scenes, the first laid in a sunlit Burgundian vineyard and opening with a charming chorus of girls gathering grapes:

Ex 41

('*Through the thick wood I went in the springtime, on a May evening*')

(And here it must be said at once that, although Kabalevsky has used only one actual French folk-tune in his score, the four-bar theme of Colas himself, he has very successfully caught the general tone of French popular music; he is at his happiest in handling this lyrical, transparent texture which suits his natural tendencies —though when dramatic feeling is called for, as in the Third Act, he rises to it with a success that astonished Russian critics.) Colas and Belette are lovers but she is also coveted by Gifflard, the

Duke's lackey. In the second scene, a fête in honour of the arrival
of the young Duke, we see Gifflard making mischief between the
lovers; he spreads a rumour that Colas is enamoured of the beautiful
Mademoiselle de Termes, who has come from Paris with the Duke;
Belette believes the story and in a fury of jealousy takes her revenge
by getting a drunken priest to marry her forthwith to Gifflard.

In the second act, a real attempt is made to show Colas as
Rolland has drawn him. In the first scene he sings, in a big aria, of
'the dark hall in the silent castle of Cuncy' whither the Duke has
carried off Colas's statue of Belette which has taken his fancy: an
attempt to sound the real depth of his character:

Ex. 42

But the suffering lover and the philosopher are soon swept away
in a drinking song; no matter what happens, life is beautiful. That is
true to the Colas of Rolland's book, and there is no doubt that the
book's unquenchable optimism was a main reason why it found

favour in the eyes of a Soviet composer and librettist.[1] Colas is joined by the curé and the notary and his sister, and the merrymaking is at its height when a terrified woman rushes in with the news that the plague has appeared in the town of Clamecy; the mood of the music changes again with absolutely Meyerbeerian theatricality and the dance tunes are succeeded by an *a cappella* chorus behind the scenes, on the *Dies irae*. The opening of the second scene of Act II corresponds to Rolland's memorable seventh chapter, 'La Peste'; Colas is sick of the plague, sick nearly to death, and quite alone. His monologue here has been compared with Mussorgsky's *Songs and Dances of Death*. He recovers, only to be faced by another catastrophe; the plague has been followed by looting and rioting, and his house, with all his masterpieces of carving, has been burned. But he remains uncrushable, and as he makes his way into the town he meets Belette, who explains why she married Gifflard and tells Colas she has loved him all the time. The music of their duet is based on themes from Act I.

Like its predecessors, the third, and last, act is in two scenes. The first shows the insurrection in Clamecy, led by one Gambi (a quite insignificant figure in Rolland's book). The rioters want to march to the castle and burn both it and the Duke, whose soldiers were responsible for bringing the plague to the town. But, much as Colas detests the tyrannical Duke, he remembers that his best carvings, including the statue of Belette, are at Cuncy; and having failed to stop the rioters he decides to warn the Duke of the approaching danger. The final scene is in the great hall at Cuncy; the song of the rebels is heard in the distance and the Duke, in a panic, is told by Gifflard that Colas is at their head; in his rage he tries to destroy Colas's masterpiece, the statue of Belette. A knock is heard; the Duke hides hurriedly; Gifflard lets in Colas and points to the

---

[1] 'The chief merit of the opera lies in the fact that, despite all its deviations from the original, it conveys the fundamental idea of Rolland's story: a man who is the master of his happiness; he boldly walks through life and reshapes it, overthrowing all obstacles in his way. This idea, the ideological leitmotive of the opera, makes it contemporary, socially significant. Far as the action is from us in time, the opera is near to us in its ideological content.' (L. Danilevich in an article on *The Master of Clamecy* in *Sovetskaya Muzika*, December 1937). But the Russian translation of Rolland's book was a remarkable best-seller in the U.S.S.R.; when Kabalevsky's choice fell on it, it had already gone into 120 editions.

mutilated statue. (The love theme from Act I is here thundered out
by the full orchestra *fff* in the manner of Mascagni.) This is the
last straw, but it fails to break Colas's back; he can still take his
revenge. Master of the situation, he throws open the gates; the
rebels pour in and the opera ends with their song of 'pike, musket,
arquebus—and *flame*'!

The Master of Clamecy was not greeted with universal praise;
Russian criticism has always been notable for its frankness, not to
say asperity, and anything less like a mutual admiration society
than the Union of Soviet Composers would be difficult to imagine.
The opera was sharply criticized mainly on account of its libretto—
particularly because of the equivocal position in which Colas is
placed between the Duke and the rioters—but also on musical
grounds: the chorus at the end of the first scene was likened by one
critic to the 'background music' of a sound-film, another complained that Kabalevsky had written a series of 'tasteful musical
water-colours' rather than an opera. But almost all acknowledged
the charm of the lyrical, transparent score and agreed that it was
the best work Kabalevsky had so far composed.

VIII. IVAN DZERZHINSKY

IVAN DZERZHINSKY enjoys the distinction of having composed a 'model' opera, a work which—despite admitted weaknesses—is officially considered to have opened a new period in the history of Soviet opera: *Quiet Flows the Don* (composed 1932–4; produced at the Leningrad Little Opera Theatre on 22 October 1935). Based on Mikhail Sholokhov's popular novel, with a libretto by the composer's brother, the work was an enormous success; it reached its 200th performance on 19 May 1938, and before this—in January 1937—a Czech version had been produced at Brno. Dzerzhinsky followed up this success by composing Sholokhov's next novel, *Virgin Soil Upturned* (produced in October 1937). In 1938 he began a third opera, *Volochaevko Days*, with a libretto by Viktor Gusev based on an episode of the Civil War in the Far East. He has, while still in his early thirties, established himself as opera-purveyor-in-chief to Soviet Russia.

Born at Tambov in 1909, Dzerzhinsky early showed considerable musical ability though he began his systematic musical education only at the age of nineteen. During 1928–30 he studied at the Gnesins' Music School in Moscow, and in the latter year went to Leningrad where, after two years at the First State Music School, he entered the Conservatoire. Here his composition professor (1932–4) was P. B. Ryazanov, a composer who has been accused of over-intellectual tendencies and of being a follower of Ravel and Stravinsky. (The second movement of his String Quartet is said to show the influence of *L'Histoire du Soldat*.) And when he left the Conservatoire Dzerzhinsky passed under the artistic tutelage of B. V. Asafiev who, if not as composer under his own name, at any rate as critic under the pseudonym 'Igor Glebov', was closely associated with the advanced modernist movement in Russia. (He was probably the leading spirit of the Association for Contemporary Music and the New Music Circle; his *Book about Stravinsky*, published in 1929, is the best monograph on its subject known to me.) It is all the more remarkable then that the pupil of Ryazanov and Asafiev should have produced, even while he was under their

influence, a work which became the model for an artistic movement
that is a reaction against everything they had stood for. As a matter
of fact some of Dzerzhinsky's earlier compositions, his music to
I. Selvinsky's *Fur Trade*, his songs (*Three Lyric Poems* and *Two
Songs of the North*) and his *Spring Suite* and *Poem about the
Dnieper* for piano, are said to show the influence of the French
impressionists and to be rather improvizatory in style. Other
streams of influence that unite in these early works are that of
Russian folksong, treated mainly in the style of Mussorgsky but
also to some extent in Grieg's, and that of Rakhmaninov's lyricism
and piano-writing—the latter more particularly in the second
movement of the First Piano Concerto.[1] In his Second Piano Concerto Dzerzhinsky, reacting strongly from Rakhmaninov 'fell into
the arms of Shostakovich' for whom, not yet in disgrace, he then
had considerable admiration. (Ironically enough the score of *Quiet
Flows the Don* is dedicated to him.) This is alleged to have had
disastrous results in the second and third movements of the Concerto, with their 'banal material, jazz episodes and instrumental
quips and cranks'; the only good movement, according to Delson, is
the first: based on folk-song and folk-dance material, some of it
actually borrowed from *Quiet Flows the Don* which was being
written at the same time.

Of Dzerzhinsky's compositions for piano solo, the *Poem about
the Dnieper* (1932; in two parts with mottoes from Gogol and
Bezïmensky, 'The Dnieper is wonderful in calm weather' and 'The
Dnieper is wonderful in all weathers when freely and easily the
mighty cranes carry concrete on the Dam') is said to be in the style
of Rakhmaninov's *Etudes-Tableaux*, the *Spring Suite* (1933; 'Idyll,'
'Song' and 'On the March!') to be in that of the early, lyrical
Prokofiev, and the *Seven Pieces* (1935) to be in the vein of Medtner's
mood pictures. According to Delson even these fairly early piano
pieces betray a weak composition-technique—and I write 'even'
advisedly; one half-expects early works to be weak technically; but
Quiet Flows the Don is itself so poor in this respect that one might
have suspected its *naïveté* to be deliberate, like the tongue-in-cheek

<hr />

[1] These criticisms are V. Delson's and are borrowed from his detailed
account of a recital of Dzerzhinsky's piano works given by the composer
himself in February 1936 (*Sovetskaya Muzika*, June 1936).

naïveté of Shostakovich's Fifth Symphony. But as a kinder critic (Budyakovsky) has put it, 'Dzerzhinsky escaped the dangers of Formalism without trouble. "Thought-out" music, the result of cogitation, is completely foreign to him—equally foreign whether in the form of the refinements of ultra-modern experiment or in that of lifeless academic schemes.' Dzerzhinsky, in short, is one of those composers who 'wish to give music as a cow gives milk'; unfortunately his milk is not Grade A.

To complete the tale of Dzerzhinsky's non-operatic compositions I must mention a set of eight *Preludes* for piano, of which I can glean no particulars, his music to a number of plays and films, and a *Russian Overture* for orchestra on which he was reported to be working two or three years ago. But these are of comparatively little account. When one thinks of Dzerzhinsky one thinks of *The Quiet Don*[1] and its successors. But before discussing these it may be worth while to listen for a moment to their composer's views on the true nature of Soviet opera;[2] 'Some composers asserted that the hero of an opera cannot be a worker or collective-farmer, as these are too "ordinary" personages. This view has been controverted in practice. Most of the heroes of most Soviet operas are simple, ordinary people whose activities are near and comprehensible to the millions who make up our Soviet audiences. Other "theorists" asserted that opera can only concern itself with profoundly personal, "lyrical" feelings and relationships, that it cannot portray social conflicts and reflect the political activity of our epoch—a theory overturned by the very existence and development of our musical culture, our musical theatre. And finally there were "theorists" who simply considered that you couldn't write anything better than the classics, and who consequently looked with extreme scepticism on the first sprouts of Soviet opera. They too have been refuted by facts. I assert that in opera one can express *everything* that is lived

---

[1] That is the real title of both novel and opera, but the popular success of the English version of the novel under the other name has given the latter the enduring stamp of familiarity.

[2] In a symposium on Soviet opera printed in *Sovetskaya Muzika* (May 1939). In the course of these remarks Dzerzhinsky referred to Knipper's *North Wind* as 'deservedly forgotten. . . . This composition, shot through with vulgar naturalism (telephone conversations, the singing of commands, etc.) is to a certain extent a vulgarization of the very idea of Soviet opera, putting a trump card into the hands of the incredulous.'

F

by the people, all the rich, living diversity of its thoughts, its moods, its struggles. But composers must know how to show all this in artistically generalized, typified figures, avoiding the pitfalls of naturalism. . . . In opera music is the chief thing, but not the only thing. The compo er should be potentially dramatist and producer as well. He should have a clear plan of the whole production, thought out to the minutest details, beginning with the music and ending with the *mise en scène*. Librettist, producer, conductor should only be auxiliaries in the realization of the idea of this complicated synthesis of the arts. . . . Soviet composers must fight against the trivial feelings, the worthless ideas, that have sometimes pervaded our young art. Our art is profoundly popular, and the people and its feelings and emotions are always great, always sublime.'

As one would expect from all this, *Quiet Flows the Don* is concerned with the relationships of individuals who can be considered typical of the masses, but it is not an 'opera without heroes' or one in which the accent is deliberately thrown on the masses as in such earlier Soviet operas as Gladkovsky's *Front and Rear*, Korchmarev's *Ten Days that Shook the World* and *The Year* 1905 by Davidenko and Shekhter. All the same, to extract a libretto from Sholokhov's long and full novel was no easy task, and the opera necessarily takes far more liberties with the book than the film did; the character of Grigory for instance is essentially changed. Thus on the one hand one is jarred by these divergencies from the novel, on the other one feels that the opera could not be fully comprehensible to anyone who had not read the book. The 'plot' extracted by Leonid Dzerzhinsky is self-contained and self-explanatory, but the characters remain sticks, lay-figures, to those who cannot clothe them with life from recollections of the novel; and his brother's music fails to clothe them with any other life. Operas based on best-sellers have, I suppose, some claim for exemption from the law that a work of art must be self-contained and self-explanatory, but I propose here to consider Dzerzhinsky's opera as it stands, not in relation to the book—which I assume the reader to know already or to be able to buy or borrow.[1] The action is laid out as follows:

Act I (Scene 1): the wedding of Grigory and Natalya, arranged

---

[1] Study of the vocal score is made the pleasanter for the English musician in that it has been thoughtfully provided with an English translation which

by their parents against the former's will; appearance of his old
love, Aksinya, who after a quarrel is knocked down by the bride's
brother, Mitka. (Scene 2): Aksinya alone; Grigory appears; they
decide to run away together. Then we see Natalya mourning her
husband's coldness, and old Melekhov, Grigory's father, trying to
comfort her. The scene ends with a general row in which Grigory
is cursed by his father, and the two lovers take to the road—like
Hugh the Drover and his sweetheart.

Act II (Scene 3): Cossacks and peasants wrangle as they wait at
a mill for their corn to be ground; Grigory and Aksinya (now
servants of a landowner, General Listnitsky) appear, followed by old
Melekhov and other Cossacks; old Melekhov quarrels with his son;
Mitka makes love to Aksinya and is knocked down by Grigory's
friend; general fight interrupted by the appearance of Listnitsky
who reads the Tsar's proclamation of war with Germany. (Scene 4):
Aksinya with her sick baby has had no news of Grigory at the front;
Listnitsky's son, Evgeny, tries to console her by making love to her;
Natalya comes with the news that Grigory has been killed.

Act III (Scene 5): At the front in 1917; some soldiers are already
mutinous but the Cossacks are still loyal; Grigory appears—he had
only been wounded—with news of the Revolution in Petrograd;
Mitka jeeringly tells him of Aksinya's faithlessness; the Cossacks
join the revolutionaries.

Act IV (Scene 6): The Listnitskys and their retainers await in
the night the attack of the revolutionaries; Grigory creeps in; scene
between him and Aksinya; Evgeny Listnitsky enters and is shot by
Grigory; the insurgent Cossacks march off to attack Novocherkassk.

And how is all this treated musically? Dzerzhinsky's music might
be summed up in a phrase as 'Mussorgsky without the flashes of
genius'; it tries to be lyrical in folk-songish style, but without
actually quoting folk-songs; it aims—in my view, quite without

surpasses in delightfulness the English texts of Haydn's oratorios and leaves
our Victorian versions of Italian opera hopelessly in the rear. I quote at
random: 'Eh, the Cossack he's well off. How'd the Cossack get such things?
From his constant pilfer . . . tfui! pelf of war'—words which, incidentally,
adhere to the music considerably less well than the Hundredth Psalm to the
tune of Greensleeves. The printed English version of Shostakovich's *The
Lady Macbeth of Mtsensk* is equally absurd and an entirely new version had
to be prepared for the concert and broadcast performance of the work in
London in March 1936.

success—at vivid and truthful declamation. But Dzerzhinsky is
strangely lacking in resource, in power of development, and in
structural ability; his stream of thought is little better than improvization, as is demonstrated most pitiably of all in the long
orchestral prelude to the last act; his texture is thin, dull and homo-
phonic; his leitmotives are crude in themselves and are never really
developed. When he borrows the conventions of classical Russian
opera (e.g. the two deaf old men in Scene 3, who correspond to
various pairs of buffoons in Borodin, Mussorgsky and Rimsky-
Korsakov) or tries to copy its strokes of peculiar genius (e.g. the
shell-shocked soldier in Scene 5, a descendant of the Idiot in
Boris), he makes nothing new of them.

Quiet Flows the Don, then, is 'official' art at very nearly its worst.
But not quite. For it has one redeeming quality not usually possessed
by official art, a quality that perhaps explains why it was approved
as a model opera for comparatively naïve listeners: it is alive. It has
melodic life; there is not one great tune in the whole work but it over-
flows with melody of an inferior, but not altogether despicable, kind
—mostly folk-songish in flavour: e.g. the hopak and Mishuk's song:

Ex.43

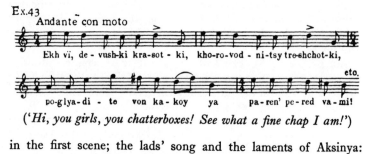

('*Hi, you girls, you chatterboxes! See what a fine chap I am!*')

in the first scene; the lads' song and the laments of Aksinya:

Ex.44

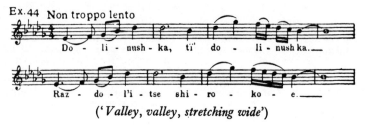

('*Valley, valley, stretching wide*')

and Natalya in the second; the peasants' chorus in the third; Aksinya's lullaby in the fourth; the orchestral theme that pervades much of the fifth scene, and the chorus of deserters. This folk-flavour is never very strong, however, and when it evaporates, the melody is sicklied over with a paler cast of lyricism and in the final chorus, 'From border to border', degenerates into a vein of forcible-feeble banality characteristic of so many of these so-called 'mass songs'.

Ex.45

Ot kra - ya i do kra - ya, ot mo - rya i do mo - rya

Among the critics of the opera was Sholokhov himself who has also told[1] how Dzerzhinsky set about the composition of an opera on his other novel *Virgin Soil Upturned*:

'Dzerzhinsky's *Quiet Flows the Don* has undoubted worth—but also serious shortcomings. Side by side with successful scenes, there is a great deal of lyrical-colourless music. The rich folklore, the marvellous Cossack songs, were not sufficiently used by the composer. However, Dzerzhinsky has learned from the criticisms of his first opera. In *Virgin Soil Upturned* the composer employs an austere, truthful musical language based on the idiom of folk-song. The music is picturesque, simple and telling. The songs, particularly the choruses, remain long imprinted in the memory. *Virgin Soil Upturned* carries Soviet opera nearly to the heights of genuine folk art.

'Dzerzhinsky, who is very talented and a hard worker, took great pains in collecting the material for this second opera. With his brother, the librettist, he visited me in a Cossack village and made himself thoroughly acquainted with the Don Cossack way of life and with the setting of my novel. He has created an important work —truthfully and artistically painting the complicated process of socialist reconstruction of the countryside of the Soviet Union. As a writer, I am satisfied with the operatic incarnation of my novel. The musical characterization of the chief characters—Lushka, Davïdov, Nagulnov and the rest—is very expressive, and despite

[1] In *Sovetskaya Muzika*, October 1937.

the fact that only these main characters of the novel appear, the
opera is a complete and finished whole. The libretto was altered
in accordance with my suggestions, and certain errors of speech
were deleted.'

To what extent this not very enthusiastic praise of Dzerzhinsky's
second opera is justified, I cannot say. The only music from it that
I know is a strophic Cossack song:

('*The regiments crossed the steppes*')

no better and no worse than similar songs in *Quiet Flows the Don*.
But judging from a lengthy analysis of the work, with music-type
examples, by A. Budyakovsky,[1] *Virgin Soil Upturned* is cut from the
same material as its predecessor: lyrical melody based on the characteristics of folksong ('not only on the intonations of the old Russian peasant songs but also on the intonations of Soviet folk-song—
in the broad sense of the word'); harmony in these lyrical passages
'extraordinarily simple, sometimes even primitive.' 'But sometimes
Dzerzhinsky's harmonic language takes on a different character,'
continues the same critic, 'it becomes hard, cutting, energetic; but
here too it is never far from the vein of Russian folk-song (as seen
through the prism of the Russian composers of the second half
of the nineteenth century, particularly Mussorgsky). Also characteristic of Dzerzhinsky is the economy of texture, the peculiar
two-part writing for the instruments. On the whole, in Dzerzhinsky's
music there is more vivid juxtaposition, tonal dislocation, repeti-
tion, than symphonic development. He is most successful in scenes
of a narrative-dramatic character. In *Virgin Soil Upturned*, as in
his other works, he very rarely employs polyphony. The four-part
choruses sometimes show their harmonic basis very clearly; not

[1] In *Sovetskaya Muzika*, October 1937.

infrequently the upper voices move in thirds. In music of folk-songish character this neglect of polyphony has a curiously negative effect; the folk-character of Dzerzhinsky's choruses comes out principally in the melodic line of the separate voices, particularly in cadences.' Polyphony, it should be explained—and polyphony not of the most primitive kind—is one of the characteristics of Russian folk-music; as a matter of fact Dzerzhinsky's choruses do sometimes remind one of Russian folk-polyphony by their tendency to come to rest on a final unison (as in the already mentioned Cossack chorus from *Virgin Soil Upturned*).

However Budyakovsky sums up that *Virgin Soil Upturned* is 'more compact, better knit than *Quiet Flows the Don* . . . the characters are much more vividly portrayed . . . the improvizatory character of Dzerzhinsky's youthful attempts is here completely outgrown.' Yet one cannot help feeling that the approval this work has won, like its predecessor, is largely due not to its musical value but to its *Weltanschauung*. The choice of this subject 'shows Dzerzhinsky's clear creative orientation. Sholokhov has a fine grasp of life. That is innate in Dzerzhinsky too. *Virgin Soil Upturned* is the first opera on the theme of Soviet country life in the period of collectivization. This difficult yet grateful theme has been developed by Dzerzhinsky with great truth and power. Musically and dramatically *Virgin Soil Upturned* is a *narodnaya opera* in the full sense of the word.[1] The simplicity and sincerity of its musical language, the lofty political sense of its theme and the realism of its artistic embodiment—these are the goals to which the Soviet composer must strive.'

Of Dzerzhinsky's third opera, *Volochaevko Days*, again I know only one number, a chorus of partisans with some novel vocal scoring (see Ex. 47 on p. 88).

The theme of the opera is once more patriotic, of that more militant type of patriotism one notices in so many Soviet compositions (and novels and poems) of the late 1930's. 'The history of the heroic struggle of the Soviet people with White Guards and foreign interventionists in the years of the Civil War abounds in remarkable episodes,' the composer has written.[2] 'Soviet

---

[1] That is, both a 'folk-opera' and a 'national opera'.
[2] *Sovetskaya Muzika*, February 1938.

('*And when the war's over!*')

patriots performed marvels of bravery in the name of love for
their fatherland. The heroic storming of Volochaevko is com-
memorated by the people in innumerable songs. But the monumental productions of Soviet musical art have not yet created
realistic images of the heroes of the Civil War. The idea of the
sacred inviolability of Soviet soil, closely and deeply touching the
heart of every citizen, strongly excites me as an artist. It gives ample
scope for the translation into musical terms of the lofty pathos of
heroism, of the sacred rage against the insolent interventionists and
of the warm patriotic enthusiasm which inspired the partisans of
the Far East as they drove out the foreign invaders. That is why
I chose as the theme of my third opera the unforgettable epic of
Volochaevko.' With what artistic success he has treated it, I cannot
say. But it is a theme on which his compatriots are performing
some notable variations.

IX. YURY SHAPORIN

YURY ALEXANDROVICH SHAPORIN is older than any of the composers I have discussed hitherto. Born at Glukhov in 1889, he stands between these younger men and the generation of their teachers: Myaskovsky and Glière and Steinberg. But like the younger men, and unlike their elders, his creative career belongs wholly to post-Revolutionary Russia. Like some of them, again, he wa late in maturing; until the age of twenty-four, when he entered the St. Petersburg Conservatoire, he had been a law student at St. Petersburg University. He remained at the Conservatoire from 1913 to 1917, studying with Sokolov, Cherepnin and Steinberg and consequently forming his style on the nationalist tradition in general and that of Rimsky-Korsakov in particular. On leaving the Conservatoire he became involved in the specialized world of the Leningrad dramatic theatres which had just passed into the control of the Revolutionary Government. Shaporin's activities at the Grand Dramatic Theatre, the Academic Theatre of Drama and other theatres—conducting, composition of incidental music, and musical advisory work in general—have doubtless been valuable to the Soviet theatre; his music to *Calm*, *The City of Winds*, *The Moon on the Left*, *The Storming of Perekop*, *Sardanapalus*, *Falstaff*, *The Straw Hat*, *The Flea* and other plays of widely different types is highly spoken of, and an orchestral suite from the last-named (1928) has passed into the concert repertoire; his film music, for *Three Songs about Lenin*, *Victory*, *The Deserter* and *Minin and Pozharsky*, is also said to be good; but one cannot help regretting its distracting effect on a man who obviously has it in him to produce music of far more permanent independent value. It is the more regrettable since Shaporin is apparently a slow worker, in marked contrast with some of his prolific younger colleagues; he took six years over his Symphony (1926–32) and his opera, *The Decembrists*, begun in 1925, was still unfinished in 1939. Almost everything he has written has been revised two or three times before publication. The list of his non-dramatic compositions is therefore very short; in addition to the works just mentioned it includes only two early

Piano Sonatas, Op.5 and Op.7 (dating from 1924 and 1927 respectively), three song-cycles on poems by Tyutchev (1926), Pushkin (1937) and Blok (1938), and, most important of all, a 'symphony-cantata' based on Blok's famous poem *On the Field of Kulikovo* (conceived at least as early as 1921 but completed only in 1938).

The piano sonatas I do not know, but L. A. Entelis[1] speaks of the composer's naturally Russian musical culture being seen in them 'through the prism of Brahms'. As a song writer Shaporin must, despite his small output, be given a high place among contemporary Russian composers. His conception of the song is essentially lyrical; his piano parts are well polished; in other words, he carries on the tradition of Rimsky-Korsakov and Tchaikovsky in song writing, not Mussorgsky's. Indeed it has been claimed for his setting of Pushkin's 'Invocation' that 'of all the songs written to this text—by Rimsky-Korsakov, Medtner, Cui, and Blumenfeld —Shaporin's comes the nearest to the poet's thought'. And, according to the same critic, his Pushkin songs as a set—there are five of them—exactly match the essential qualities of Pushkin's lyricism: 'crystal clearness and depth of thought, finely wrought structure.'

But it is on three major works that Shaporin's reputation really rests: the Symphony, *On the Field of Kulikovo* and the unfinished but much discussed *Decembrists*. The Symphony has been heard once in this country; it was broadcast from Queen's Hall on 23 January 1935, Albert Coates conducting, and, except Shostakovich's Seventh, is so far the only specimen of the 'monumental' type of Soviet symphony with which we are acquainted. On that occasion the predominant feeling among the audience was, unless I am mistaken, disappointment: for one thing, the result seemed hardly proportionate to the vast means employed (chorus, orchestra, and brass band), and there was a curious sense of disillusionment at the discovery that Revolutionary Russia could produce such far from revolutionary music. It was Borodin inflated to the dimensions of Mahler; and as there was some genuine Borodin, the B minor Symphony, in the same programme we felt this was no improvement. Whether or not we were right in our judgment of the Symphony, measured by absolute values; whether or not there is

[1] Article on Shaporin in the booklet *Sovetskie Kompozitori* (Leningrad Philharmonia, 1938).

some element in the make-up of most British musicians which
blinds us to the beauties of the monumental in music (we have little
use for Bruckner or Mahler and many of us make certain reserva-
tions in our admiration for even Beethoven's Ninth and the great
Schubert C major); in any case we were wrong on one important
point—we were, if only unconsciously, condemning Shaporin for
not hitting a mark that he was not aiming at. What he really was
aiming at, we did not understand—and so were not in a position to
judge of his success. But understanding of this point is absolutely
essential to the formation of a just appreciation not only of
Shaporin's Symphony but of all these other 'epic' or 'monumental' symphonies that I have been describing, indeed of the
great bulk of Soviet music in general. This is music written not for
beauty's sake, not to delight and interest a more or less sophisticated
audience; it is music written to impress musically unsophisticated
(however naturally musical) masses and to inspire them with definite
ideals. We may deplore the deliberate *naïveté* of much of this
music, feeling that it is not quite natural to the composers; we may
deplore the limitations imposed on creative artists by a government,
however kindly disposed to the arts, which has a monopoly of
publishing and hence the power of life and death over all art
created under its jurisdiction. But we must also remember that the
Soviet authorities in giving these 'directives', and the Soviet composers in obeying them, are following an almost traditional line in
Russian aesthetics, a line (that the true purpose of art is social or
moral) which can be traced back through Tolstoy and *What is Art?*
to the mid-nineteenth-century critics Chernïshevsky, Dobrolyubov
and Pisarev. Shaporin's Symphony and its kind are fulfilments of
Tolstoy's prophecy about 'the art of the future'. 'Art of the future,'
he wrote, 'will consist not in transmitting feelings accessible only
to members of the rich classes, as is the case to-day, but in transmitting feelings embodying the highest religious perception of our
times'. (By which he does not mean 'religious' in the orthodox
sense.) 'Only those productions will be esteemed art which transmit
feelings drawing men together in brotherly union, or such universal
feelings as can unite all men. Only such art will be chosen, tolerated,
approved, and diffused.' And in Soviet Russia it is so. Shaporin's
Symphony was written for Tolstoy's ideal listener (and reader and

looker-at-pictures) 'the peasant of unperverted taste'; we listened
to it in 1935 with ears 'perverted' by music more sophisticated than
Tolstoy ever dreamed of in his worst nightmares. We could not,
and cannot, do otherwise; but unless we can make *some* adjustment
of our aural perspective we can never hope to appreciate Soviet
music justly. And Shaporin, unlike Dzerzhinsky, is a good enough
musician to repay us for the effort.

To return to the Symphony itself: according to the composer,[1]
it is an attempt 'to show the development of the fate of a human
being in a great historical upheaval. It portrays the gradual transformation of individual consciousness in the progress of acceptance
of the Revolution.' What Shaporin did not tell his correspondent
was the history of the gradual transformation of a musical composition 'in the progress of acceptance of the Revolution'; for the Symphony was originally conceived as a piano concerto, an embryonic
stage which accounts for the episodic piano solo in the finale. In its
existing form, however, the Symphony consists of four movements
entitled 'What Actually Happened',[2] 'Dance,' 'Lullaby' and
'Campaign'. The first, with its more or less declamatory opening,
is the most subjective, the most nearly autobiographical part of the
Symphony. The principal second-subject idea—treated as a theme
with three variations for chorus and orchestra, on the lines of the
parallel passage in Brahms's C minor Piano Quartet—is the song,
'Little Apple', which enjoyed great popularity in the days of what
is now known as 'militant communism' (i.e. the Revolution and
Civil War); it has been used symbolically more than once in Soviet
music, for instance in Glière's ballet *The Red Poppy*, where it
figures—again as theme-and-variations—as the 'Dance of the Soviet
Sailors', and in Gladkovsky's opera *Front and Rear*; but whereas
Glière preserves the simple 2/4 character of the tune throughout:

Ex.48

Pesante

----

[1] Letter to Slonimsky, quoted in *Music since* 1900.
[2] *Bil*, which has been translated 'The Past' (it is connected with the past
tense of the verb 'to be'), here means 'a fact', 'a true story'.

Shaporin has twisted it into a whimsical rhythmic pattern:

Ex. 49   etc.

On the whole, however, the first movement is built on fairly orthodox lines, with a shortened recapitulation. The brilliant 'Dance' and the 'Lullaby' for female chorus and orchestra correspond to the normal scherzo and slow movement, and it is not easy to relate them to the composer's process of 'accepting the Revolution'. But the 'monumental' last movement, 'Campaign,' with its march-rhythms, its independent brass band answering the orchestral brass, its massive choruses and its introduction of another popular Civil War tune, 'Budyonny's March', must be very nearly ideal revolutionary music. Not quite, for even here there are Rakhmaninov-like episodes:

Ex. 50
Andante, molto espressivo

Indeed the Symphony as a whole has been criticized[1] for its 'static quality in showing the revolutionary process, its mechanical juxtaposition of the personal world of the individual with the elemental strength of the movement of colossal human masses. The personality is not so much re-orientated in the process of struggle and active participation, as pushed aside by the mighty movement of the collective mass. . . . The concluding mass song is insufficiently prepared by all the preceding development.' Nor, I may add, is it a very good tune:

---

[1] By Ostretsov in *Sovetskaya Muzika*, April 1935.

Ex 51

A more artistic, less ideological judgment is that by Bogdanov-Berezovsky,[1] who drawing attention to Shaporin's musical ancestry —'Mussorgsky's intonations, Borodin's rhythms, Rakhmaninov's cantabile melodies, Rimsky-Korsakov's orchestral layout'—also acutely points out the relation of the Symphony to other 'Slavonic monuments', 'to the paintings of Roerikh, to the Scythian and Slavonic motives in the poetry of Blok (e.g. *The Scythians, On the Field of Kulikovo*)'.

That was very astute indeed if Bogdanov-Berezovsky did not know that Shaporin had long had his eye on the last-named poem (or, rather, cycle of five poems). His setting of it seems to be generally regarded as his masterpiece and one of the supreme masterpieces of Soviet music. Blok's poem, written in 1908,[2] is a mystical meditation—shot through with prophetic hints—on one of Russia's most famous medieval battlefields: the plain of Kulikovo, where in 1380 Dmitry Donskoy overthrew the Tartars and sealed the unity of the North Russian principalities. As the historian Klyuchevsky has remarked in a sentence which appears on the title page of Shaporin's score: 'The Russian State was born not in the money chest of Ivan Kalita but on the field of Kulikovo.' The other epigraph on the score is equally significant; 'The Russians, by checking the invasion of the Mongols, saved European civilization'; it is significant, that is to say, of the re-orientation of Russian thought that was taking place in the late 1930's, while Shaporin was composing this work, away from communist internationalism and towards patriotic Russianness—obviously in reaction to the growing

[1] *Sovetskaya Muzika*, June 1934.
[2] There is an English translation by C. Fillingham Coxwell in Russian Poems (C. W. Daniel, 1929). The Russian text is given in the *Oxford Book of Russian Verse*, where an editorial note tells us that 'the poem is a lyrical "variation" on the theme of an Old-Russian prose-poem' on the battle.

menace of Nazidom. Shaporin's *Kulikovo* (1938) and Prokofiev's
Alexander Nevsky (1939) are both symptoms of this tendency;
instead of glorifying the Revolution, they glorify Russia's heroic
age.

Shaporin has always been fond of history—as we shall see in a
moment, his only opera is on a historical subject—and it is said
that before composing *Kulikovo* he studied all the not inconsider-
able literature on the battle. He has not set Blok's poem just as it
stands; in collaboration first with the poet himself until his death
in 1921, then with M. Lozinsky, he has 'based on the material of
Blok's verses a real dramatic libretto with concrete characters and
a consistent, logical argument', and set it for four soloists (soprano,
mezzo, tenor, bass), chorus and orchestra. This sounds rather
cantata-like, indeed the work is styled a 'symphony-cantata', and
that exactly describes its nature; it is an interesting attempt to
'cross' these two forms. There are movements in sonata-form (the
prologue, the scene of the battle) and passages in quasi-operatic
forms (Dmitry's monologue in the prologue, and the 'Bride's
Cavatina'); the 'Ballad of the Knight' is a theme with variations;
the great choral scene 'In the night when Mamay lay with his
host' is cast as a sonata-rondo. *On the Field of Kulikovo* is in fact
just as much a symphony as its ancestor, Berlioz's *Roméo et
Juliette*. There are eight movements in all. The prologue opens
with a powerful, rather Borodinesque unison passage:

Ex.52

symbolic of Mamay and the Tartar host and recurring as a motto-
theme throughout, but the music soon changes to the mood of
Blok's lines which are then sung by the chorus (a picture of the
flowing Don and the wide steppes) and continued in a sort of
dialogue between Dmitry Donskoy and the chorus (the prince's
call for unity against the invader). The second movement, the
'Bride's Cavatina', a Russian girl's fears for her warrior betrothed,
is based on another poem of Blok's rewritten by him for Shaporin

just before his death; Shaporin's setting is of great beauty—and there
is no reason why it should not be sung as a separate concertaria:

Ex. 53

('*In the days when the leaves fall*')

Next come the already mentioned chorus developed from the
third of the Blok poems, 'In the night when Mamay lay with
his host', and the 'Ballad of the Knight', based on Blok's fourth
poem, a picture of the Russian warrior which is a sort of companion-
piece to the cavatina, a picture of Russian womanhood. The
variation-treatment of the ballad is striking; the theme is stated
by the orchestra only, the voice entering in the first variation.
The fifth movement is another great choral scene, a battle picture
for which Blok wrote special words not in his original poem; the
'Tartar' theme from the opening of the prologue plays a prominent
part and the anonymous 'knight' of the previous movement is also
to the fore. (On the whole he is made a more important figure than
Prince Dmitry; he is the male symbol of the Russian people—and
the symphony is meant to glorify the people, rather than the
Prince.) After the battle scene comes a lullaby for mezzo-soprano,
chorus and orchestra: mother and children weep for the husband
and father fallen in fight; the words are (I think) from a folk-song,
at any rate not by Blok, and the music is very simple and expressive.
Another interpolation, a chorus of 'messengers' (including the
symbolic knight), concludes the historic portion of the work with
triumphant fanfares. There remains the epilogue of the present-day,

based on Blok's fifth and last poem, 'Again on the field of Kulikovo', rounding off the work musically by gathering up the
thematic threads and pointing the patriotic moral. For whereas
Blok had ended in 1908 on a prophetic note: 'Not for nothing are
the clouds gathering. . . . Thy hour has struck. Pray!' Shaporin
and Lozinsky have given the poem a more militant ending: 'The
storm is approaching. . . . Take courage, brothers! The hour is near!'

In giving so much space to *Kulikovo*, perhaps the finest musical
work Soviet Russia has yet produced, despite its reliance on the
idiom of the last-century Nationalists, I have left myself little room
to discuss the opera, *The Decembrists*. But *The Decembrists*, when
last heard of, was still unfinished; one version had been completed
by 1938 but Shaporin was dissatisfied with it and drastically revised
it. The libretto, by the novelist Alexey N. Tolstoy,[1] is based on the
historic incident of the attempted *coup d'état* of the Liberal Con-
stitutionalists in December 1825, and the heroine, Pauline Annen-
kova, was a real person, a French shop-girl who distinguished
herself by the devotion with which she followed her exiled husband
to Eastern Siberia, nursed him through illness and kept up his
courage during eighteen weary years; she died only in 1876. The
opera shows the love of Pauline and Annenkov against the social
and political background of Annenkov's home—his mother is an
aristocratic landowner of the worst type—and of the ideals and
fate of the Decembrists. Judging from such excerpts as Pauline's
aria in the second scene:

Ex. 54

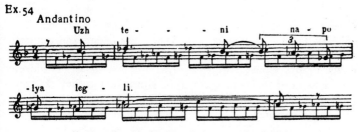

('*Already the shadows lay upon the fields*')

[1] Not to be confused with the great nineteenth-century poet, Alexey K.
Tolstoy, who in turn has been taken by at least one English writer on
Tchaikovsky to be the author of *War and Peace* and *Anna Karenina*.

G

and the orchestral introduction to the third:

Ex. 55

the score is a curiously satisfactory synthesis of those seeming incompatibles, Mussorgsky and Tchaikovsky. One only misses—and of course it is a very serious lack—some element that can be isolated and labelled 'unmistakable Shaporin'. Shaporin is an epigone; but he is an epigone of very great talent, and moreover a talent of such a nature that it is not embarrassed by the artistic policy of the Soviet Government. There are doubtless cleverer and more individual composers in the U.S.S.R., but they are handicapped in the race. The only limitations from which Shaporin suffers are personal ones.

INDEX